How to Pass the Civil Service Qualifying Tests

The essential guide for clerical and Fast Stream applications

Mike Bryon

4th edition

KoganPage

LONDON PHILADELPHIA NEW DELH

Whilst the author has made every effort to ensure that the content of this book is accurate, please note that occasional errors can occur in books of this kind. If you suspect that an error has been made in any of the tests included in this book, please inform the publishers at the address printed below so that it can be corrected at the next reprint.

Publisher's note

Every possible effort has been made to ensure that the information contained in this book is accurate at the time of going to press, and the publishers and author cannot accept responsibility for any errors or omissions, however caused. No responsibility for loss or damage occasioned to any person acting, or refraining from action, as a result of the material in this publication can be accepted by the editor, the publisher or the author.

First published in Great Britain in 1995 by Kogan Page Limited
Reprinted 1997, 1998, 1999
Second edition 2003
Reprinted 2003, 2005
Third edition 2007
Reprinted 2008, 2009 (twice)
Fourth edition 2010

Kogan Page Limited
120 Pentonville Road
London N1 9JN
United Kingdom
www.koganpage.com

British Library Cataloguing in Publication Data

A CIP record for this book is available from the British Library.

ISBN   978 0 7494 6179 9
E-ISBN   978 0 7494 6180 5

Typeset by Graphicraft Limited, Hong Kong
Printed and bound in India by Replika Press Pvt Ltd

Contents

Preface

Use this book to find your way successfully through the initial stages of the UK Civil Service Ordinary entry or Fast Steam recruitment process. It has been developed expressly for the purpose of helping prepare for the Civil Service qualifying exams.

This edition has been completely updated. It contains harder practice questions. There is new material on online tests, on following procedure, on speed and accuracy, situational tests, personality and attitudinal questionnaires, as well as e-tray exercises, written exercises and assessment days. It offers well over 100 tips and insights into the Fast Stream competition and, in response to readers' requests, provides more and fuller explanations.

If you are about to take a Civil Service test, first establish that the practice questions contained here are indeed relevant to the test that you face. The department or agency to which you have applied should have directed you to a description of its test and a number of sample questions. It is essential that you study this information carefully and, before you spend time on these exercises, establish that this material is relevant to the real questions. This book is a learning aid and contains material intended to help you reach the standard demanded by the real tests and master the competencies tested in them. To aid learning, sections usually start with questions easier than those found in the real test.

To do well in Civil Service tests, many people need to set about quite a major programme of revision. You may need more practice material than is contained in this book. There are many other good sources, some online as well as other books. If you are finding it difficult to identify sufficient relevant practice material, then by all means e-mail me at help@mikebryon.com, providing details of the Civil Service test that you face and an e-mail address at which you can be contacted. I will be glad to inform you of any other source that I know.

I apologize in advance if you discover any errors in these practice questions; try not to allow it to undermine your confidence in the value of practice and please do not take too dim a view of the rest of the book, because it definitely does contain lots of worthwhile practice material. I have tried hard to keep errors out and I hope I have not missed too many. I will be glad to hear of any, care of Kogan Page, in order that they can be removed at the next reprint.

Acknowledgements

The first edition of this book was written with the encouragement and support of staff from the Recruitment and Assessment Services, at that time a department of the Cabinet Office. Previous editions have helped tens of thousands of applicants to prepare for the Civil Service qualifying tests. The idea formed over 15 years ago and came from my work for departments of the Civil Service supporting many hundreds of candidates in their applications to the service. If you find this book helpful, it is because of the insights provided to me by those individuals, many of whom are now working in the service. I am indebted to them. The Civil Service tests are in an almost constant state of development and I am also indebted to the many readers who have contacted me for advice when new styles of test and question appear.

The views expressed are not those of the government, any department of the Civil Service or any serving civil servant. The practice questions are not from past papers and are not real Civil Service exam questions; they and the advice offered have been written and used to help real candidates pass the real tests. Any errors or omissions are entirely mine.

May I take this opportunity to wish you every success in your attempt to join the Civil Service, and in particular in meeting the challenge of the qualifying tests.

Mike Bryon – A pioneer in test coaching

Employers used to argue that candidates could not improve their score in psycho-metric tests. Mike Bryon proved otherwise. It is now unanimously acknowledged that every candidate can improve how they perform in these common selection tools.

Mike Bryon was first published in 1991 and now has 17 books in print on how to pass the tests and assessments used by large employers. He is the best-selling author on the subject. Each book contains advice on the winning mindset, insights and tips, hundreds of realistic example questions, practice tests, answers, explanations and interpretations of your score. Hundreds of thousands of people have used the books to get down to some serious score improving practice and succeed in the test and assessments they face. The books have sold worldwide and have been translated into many foreign languages including Indonesian, Portuguese, Russian, Polish, Indian and Chinese.

After three years of postgraduate research into adult learning at the University of Birmingham (UK) he founded a consultancy and for 15 years he provided recruit-ment and diversity consultancy to organizations in every industrial sector and a great many major UK and international companies including Departments of the UK Government, national utilities, high-street retail chains, rail companies, local and emergency authorities, and multinationals such as the Ford Motor Company and British Airport Authorities. The consultancy contributed extensively to EU research programmes with research partners drawn from across the union.

His books review the strategies and provide the practice you need to gain a competitive advantage. Importantly they offer practice at a level that reflects that of the actual tests. These books really do offer hundreds of realistic practice questions; usually 400 or 500. Many of the titles offer far more than this. *Ultimate Psychometric Tests* (£9.99) contains over 1,000 practice questions and is perfect for the candidate who faces tests at the intermediate level or seeks an introduction to graduate material.

The titles reach across the whole testing spectrum from intermediate through to graduate and the high flyer. There is winning advice, insights and tips on personality questionnaires, situational awareness tests, assessment days, group exercises, role plays and in-tray or e-tray exercises. There are books to help candidates who dare to dream of a single career goal, including applicant firefighters, candidates for the UK Civil Service (including the Fast Stream), postgraduate business school applicants who face the GMAT and medical school applicants who face the UKCAT. Mike Bryon has also written on secondary transfer for children of 11 years of age, and adults who face a test as speakers of English as a second language.

Mike Bryon has over 10 years of experience in the training room, making sure every candidate demonstrates their full potential and realizes the career of their choice. His groundbreaking approach has proved decisive for countless thousands of candidates.

His work remains contemporary through his continual research and writing and through the many readers who contact him for advice and suggestions on sources of practice questions. During your programme of review, if you hit a problem or if you would like suggestions of sources of practice material then e-mail Mike Bryon at: help@mikebryon.com.

CHAPTER 1

The Civil Service, the tests and practice

Administrative staff in the Civil Service

Why is it that people routinely work to improve their CV or interview technique, but few seek to improve their performance in employers' tests?

This book is packed with insights and practice questions. Use it to fulfil your dream of winning a vital and influential position within the Civil Service.

Too few candidates realize that they can improve their scores in these common assessments. Occupational psychologists accept that a lack of familiarity with tests, low self-esteem, nervousness or a lack of confidence will result in a lower score. It is equally true to say that hard work, determination and, most of all, systematic preparation can lead to a significant improvement in performance. For some candidates, practice will mean the difference between passing and failing.

Civil servants are officials who work for a minister of the government of the day. They work in departments and agencies of central government, developing and implementing policies. Employees of the police, local government and the armed services are not civil servants.

Civil servants are politically impartial and the service is non-political. Governments change but the service remains unaffected and will serve whichever government is elected.

Administrators in the service are in an important respect considered to be generalists. After a qualifying period, and once you reach the higher grades, you may gain experience of all aspects of administration and move between specialist functions periodically. The experience gained from each function is considered to be transferable, and you will be expected to be able to learn quickly and to be flexible. Training is primarily on the job. In recent years the service has undergone considerable change; structures used to be centrally defined but this no longer necessarily applies throughout the service. Increasingly, civil servants are occupied with the development and implementation of the policies of the European Union as well as those of Parliament.

A major effort has been made to locate parts of departments and most of the executive agencies outside the capital. This has meant that fewer civil servants are located in London and the South-East region generally.

Another change has been the provision of information about the service and vacancies on the internet. This is a vital source of information, especially in terms of the type of work available and the recruitment process, including any tests. The internet makes it far easier to keep the information up to date and provides a very cost-effective means of providing a great deal of information. There is little point in attempting to repeat or summarize this material here. See 'Further information' for useful web addresses.

Up until now, the terms and conditions of employment of civil servants have been explained in a substantial, rigorous and clearly written publication called *The Civil Service Staff Handbook*. Although, in recent years, the prospects of promotion have reduced considerably, all staff benefit from annual appraisals, which include an assessment of whether or not they are 'fit' for promotion.

It is a legal requirement that recruitment to the service is by fair and open competition and that selection and promotion are on the basis of merit alone. Fairness and openness mean that the service is required to ensure that vacancies are widely publicized, and this often results in very large numbers of applications. To ensure fairness, each applicant must be given proper and due consideration, which takes a considerable amount of time and resources.

The process used to recruit to the service usually comprises most or all of the following features:

1 Applicants are referred to information about the vacancies and departments. The intention is to allow candidates to make an informed decision over whether or not to proceed with their application.

2 Self-assessments are used to further help applicants to decide if they are suited to the service.

3 Through an application form, sufficient information is obtained to sift the candidates on the basis of a set of criteria agreed in advance and considered

essential to the post. It is common for many candidates to be rejected at this stage, so take care to present your experience as relevant, and minimize the number of errors on your form.

4 One questionnaire or a series of questionnaires may be used that ask questions about your working style and personality. These are used to determine whether candidates are suited to a career in the service.

5 Applicants may have to pass a set of standardized tests, which are administered either online or to large groups of applicants.

6 The next stage in the process may include an e-tray exercise. This is a type of work-sample test that resembles a Microsoft Outlook® inbox containing background files and which receives a series of 'e-mails' to which the candidate must respond.

7 Candidates who have successfully passed the sift stages may be required to attend an assessment centre where they undertake work-related exercises, discussion groups, written assignments, interviews and the preparation and delivery of a presentation.

8 Panel interviews are conducted.

The service is an acknowledged leader in the field of providing childcare support, career-break schemes and job-sharing arrangements. I have first-hand experience of working with civil servants who take equality of opportunity very seriously and work hard to ensure a fair and equitable system of recruitment and management.

There have been considerable and genuine efforts, coordinated by the Cabinet Office, to address issues of representation.

The Cabinet Office continually monitors the service's recruitment processes, including the qualifying exams, for bias, and takes measures to guard against any unintentional racial or gender discrimination. No system is perfect, but candidates should take some assurance from the fact that the service is ahead of the majority of British businesses in operating a relatively equitable recruitment process, and in this respect represents a better employer than most.

A programme of validity studies is carried out to demonstrate that the selected candidates go on to be successful in the Civil Service.

The *Fast Stream Report 2005* found that candidates who described their ethnicity as black or as belonging to an ethnic minority group were disproportionately unsuccessful at the qualifying test stage and that people with a disability were successful in broadly the same proportions as they applied, but only a small number applied in the first instance.

Tests and practice

Let's deal with a few still common misconceptions. If you fail one of the Civil Service qualifying tests, it does not mean that you lack the potential to be a civil servant. The tests do not test your innate ability, and you can markedly improve your score through practice. Most successful candidates have practised before they take a Civil Service test. Many pass them only after two or more attempts. Most go on to prove themselves to be very able civil servants.

When tests are used to select and reject applicants, they leave you as a candidate with no alternative but to try to earn the very best possible score. When there are lots of candidates and relatively few vacancies, then, like it or not, you have entered a competition – in many instances a fierce competition. You must do better than most other candidates in order to be selected for the next stage in the recruitment process.

Two things will help you succeed. First, realize that practice prior to the test is essential if you are to become familiar with the test demands, build up speed and avoid common mistakes. Second, you must realize that doing well in a test is not simply down to intelligence; you must also be sufficiently motivated to want to pass and to try very hard, both before the test and during the test itself. In some cases, practice and a determination to do well will mean you succeed when you would otherwise have not.

All employers' tests, including those used by the Civil Service, owe much of their heritage to attempts early in the last century to measure intelligence. We are all familiar with the notion of IQ (intelligence quotient) and how a score is offered as a measurement of an individual's intelligence: for example, a score of 100 is deemed average, while a score of over 160 might indicate genius. Pioneers of testing predicted that we would no longer have to wait for the lessons of experience to discover how well suited anybody was for a particular career or educational path. Instead we would be able to attribute scores to individuals and be able to tell who was best suited for a particular career or for a place in, for example, higher education.

It was soon realized that these early tests failed to predict success in particular careers or higher education. Intelligence is a complex and controversial notion that has proved very difficult to define. The concept of intelligence adopted by the early testers was crude and related to only a few of the items that affect the complexities of understanding intelligence. The early tests were primarily concerned with the measurement of verbal ability and the handling of numerical, pictorial and geometric relations.

The validity of these early tests was much exaggerated, and this gave rise to considerable scepticism and some hostility towards testing. There had, of course, been more sober commentators, and the views of these individuals came to the fore. In particular, it was stressed that someone's score should be taken not as an indication of overall intelligence, but simply as a measurement of that individual's ability in the aptitude tested. Some IQ tests were renamed ability tests and redesigned to measure single aptitudes more specifically. Instead of attributing a single score, tests offered a profile of scores in various abilities. In other cases an individual's score was compared with the normal score of other candidates with similar backgrounds. These tests are in essence the precursors of the tests used today by employers. Considerable and lengthy studies are undertaken in order to quantify the predictive value of such tests.

Today these tests are written by occupational psychologists who go to considerable lengths to achieve objectivity by applying standard scientific methods and statistical techniques to the task of deciding between candidates. This is not to say that the tests are perfect; in fact the vast majority are not. However, the resulting psychometric scores are considered by many to be the best single predictor of likely job performance.

Notification that you have been unsuccessful may mean nothing more than that you did not do well enough in the competition on that occasion. You should certainly not conclude that failure to pass a qualifying exam means that you are unsuitable for employment as a civil servant. In some instances so many people apply and there are so few vacancies that even very able candidates are rejected. So do not immediately rethink your career plans. Try again after doing more practice. If you repeatedly fail, try to establish if any alternative routes exist into the employment of your choice. It may be that holders of particular qualifications do not have to sit the exam, or you may be able to join the department at a more junior grade and seek promotion.

A winning approach

The best frame of mind in which to approach a qualifying exam is to treat it as an opportunity to demonstrate your true worth. Avoid any feelings of resentment over the fact that you have to take a test. Do not fear failure but instead concentrate on the opportunity to pass. Have confidence in yourself. Realize that you have nothing to lose if you try your best and really go for it.

Practice before a qualifying exam is essential, and can make a significant difference to your score. It is obvious that practice will help. It will mean that you make fewer mistakes and work more quickly against the often tight time constraints. It will ensure you are familiar with the test demands, and that you revise forgotten rules and develop a good test technique.

If passing is important to you, you should be prepared to make a major commitment in terms of setting time aside to practise during the weeks leading up to the test. You can be sure that other candidates will make such a commitment, so you risk coming a poor second if you do not. To maximize the benefits of practice you should undertake two types of exercise:

1 Warm-up practice. You should practise in a relaxed situation, without time constraints, on questions that are similar to those described in the department's test. The aim is to realize the test demands and work out why you got a question wrong. This way you revise the competencies and build up confidence in your own abilities.

2 Realistic test practice against the clock. Now practise on realistic questions against a strict time limit and in circumstances as similar to the test as you can manage. The aim is to get used to answering the questions under the pressure of time and to build up speed and accuracy.

Practise on as much material as you can obtain, but restrict your practice to questions similar to the real thing.

CHAPTER 2

Practice for the administrative grades

I used this book to understand and appreciate what is required to pass the tests for ordinary entry. It's a must for anyone trying to get in.
READER REVIEW

Considerable decentralization has taken place in recruitment to the Civil Service. In the 1990s, uniform nationwide procedures were applied in every department or agency. Today only selection for the Fast Stream is done through a national test, with departments and agencies adopting their own procedures for recruitment to all other grades. This said, most departments continue to use a recruitment process that broadly comprises three features – application sifting, tests and panel interviews – and there is still considerable similarity in the competencies examined across all departments and agencies.

Most vacancies will be advertised through government websites, local papers and job centres. More senior grades such as executive officers may be advertised on the public-service day in the national press, for example *The Guardian* (on Wednesdays) and journals such as *New Scientist*.

Your work as an administrator in the Civil Service is likely to consist of tasks such as dealing with customers, operating computer systems and updating records, financial administration, procurement, marketing or public relations.

If you join as an administrative assistant, you will be involved in general clerical duties and could be filing and looking after official papers and documents, or writing straightforward letters. You may also be involved in receiving and dispatching correspondence, photocopying and distributing documents, or answering and making telephone calls.

Responsibilities for administrative officers may include: preparing documentation in accordance with guidance, researching and collating information, updating computer data and maintaining accurate records, writing reports, and the supervision of administrative assistants.

If you're already at middle or senior management level, then consider applying for a position as an executive officer. This role focuses on people management and duties such as coordinating large-scale clerical exercises, organizing training and assisting in business management.

Tests are often used in the recruitment to these grades; they may be online or you may be asked to sit a paper-and-pen version. If you have never taken a psychometric test before, then to get some idea of what to expect think back to the days of examinations, and in particular SATs (short-answer tests) at school. The qualifying exams for the Civil Service are almost certain to consist of multiple-choice or short-answer questions, and you must compete for one of the places against other candidates.

If you are invited to attend a test centre, you will face either a room set out as an examination hall with small desks, or banks of computer terminals, depending on whether you face a paper-and-pen or computer-administered version of the test. Other candidates are very likely to be present. In some instances there may be a lot of them. A test administrator will welcome you and explain the process. They will be following a prepared script, and will be happy to answer any questions, although the answers given may be rather brief or superficial. This is because the administrator is keen that all candidates (including those who attend on a different day and will not have heard your question) receive the same information and experience the same test conditions, so they will be reluctant to stray far from the script.

Whether you face a test online or at a test centre, if you suffer a disability that may affect your performance and means you require things to be organized in a different way, then contact the department or agency straight away.

The types of practice question in this chapter

The following questions are characteristic of the type used to recruit to the administrative grades described above. But check their relevance to the particular test that you face before you spend time working through the material. While the next chapter provides further questions under practice test conditions, this chapter offers practice in the following types of question:

- handling data: the essentials (38 questions);

- quantitative reasoning (29 questions);

- data interpretation (34 questions);

- word swap (19 questions);

- missing words (21 questions);

- correct sentences (20 questions);

- following procedures (10 questions);

- speed and accuracy (23 questions).

To maximize the benefit of practice, you may need more material than is contained in this volume. Sources of other suitable practice material in the Kogan Page testing series include:

- *The Numeracy Test Workbook*;

- *How to Pass Numeracy Tests*;

- *How to Pass Numerical Reasoning Tests: A Step by Step Approach to the Key Skills*;

- *Ultimate Psychometric Tests*;

- *How to Pass Verbal Tests*;

- *How to Pass Selection Tests*.

In some tests for the Civil Service you are allowed a calculator, but even so don't risk taking a real test unless you have revised your mental arithmetic. For this reason I suggest that you do not use a calculator to answer the following questions (but by all means use one to check your answers or when trying to work out where you have gone wrong).

Handling data: the essentials

You should be able to answer these questions without a calculator in under 30 seconds. Once you manage that, you should practise some more until you can answer them in 15 seconds! So get practising. There is no better way than practice to improve your speed and accuracy in this key competency.

Try the following 38 questions.

1   Orlando is facing south. If he turns through one right angle anticlockwise, in which direction will he face?

Answer

2   Allegra is facing north and turns through three right angles in a clockwise direction. In what direction does she now face?

Answer

3   Greg turns through two right angles in a clockwise direction. He ends up facing south. In which direction was he originally facing?

Answer

4   David is lost. He set off this morning walking due west and from the sun's position can tell that he is now facing due east. He knows he made two right-angled turns. Can you tell if he turned clockwise or anticlockwise from the information given?

Answer

5   A store sells batteries for £3.00 for a pack of four. What is the cost of each battery?

Answer

6   A store sells batteries for £3.00 for a pack of four. How many batteries will you get for £21?

Answer

7   A shop sells batteries for £1.33 each. How much will four cost?

Answer

8   A shop sells batteries for £1.50. What is the cost of 12?

Answer

9   A supermarket needs 48 till rolls for a usual Saturday's trading. The rolls come in packs of three. How many packs will the store use on a typical Saturday?

Answer

10   Eggs are sold in boxes of six for £1.56. How much would 24 eggs cost?

Answer

11   Eggs are sold in boxes of six for £1.56. How much would 20 eggs cost? (Assume that the store will split a box.)

Answer [   ]

12   A medium-sized egg weighs 60 g. How much do six weigh?

Answer [   ]

13   If six eggs weigh in total 300 g, how much would you expect four of them to weigh?

Answer [   ]

14   Lola raised £132 for charity by giving sponsored Italian language lessons. She charges £12 a lesson, so how many lessons did she give?

Answer [   ]

15   Hope was sponsored 30p for each length that she swam. She raised a total of £12.00. How many lengths did she manage to swim?

Answer [   ]

16   A kilo of Parmesan cheese costs £16.00. How much would a piece that weighed 550 g cost?

Answer [   ]

17   400 g of beans comprises 1,600 beans. How much does each bean weigh?

Answer [   ]

18   Ten heaps each contain 37 individual beans, and each bean has an average weight of 0.3 g. How much do all the beans weigh (ie all the beans in all the heaps)?

Answer [   ]

19   Douglas purchased 25 kilos of potatoes at 28p a kilo. How much did he spend?

Answer [   ]

20   An electricity bill is calculated by a charge of 10.1p for each unit of power used. How much would the charge be if you had used 660 units?

Answer [   ]

21   The tax on electricity charges of £48.00 is 5 per cent. How much tax will be added to the charge?

Answer

22   Twenty per cent of men responded positively when asked whether or not they hated Mondays. If the total survey comprised 60 men, how many responded positively to the question?

Answer

23   At a bus terminus, one bus is scheduled to arrive every three minutes. How many should arrive during a four-hour shift?

Answer

24   Ella counted 30 aeroplanes going over her house in a six-hour period. How many minutes separated each plane? (Assume the intervals were equal.)

Answer

25   On the day of the train drivers' strike, 13 staff out of a workforce of 39 arrived at work late. What percentage of the workers were late that day?

Answer

26   If this exercise comprised a total of 45 questions and you were allowed 10 seconds to attempt each, how long would the exercise last?

Answer

27   Nine people ate at a restaurant and agreed to share the bill equally. The bill came to £202.50. How much did each have to contribute?

Answer

28   You agreed to pay half the cost of a carpet for a room with an area of four square metres at a cost of £30 per square metre. What is the value of your contribution?

Answer

29   You have agreed to a 12 per cent service charge on a bill of £112. How much extra will the cost be?

Answer

30 Tax is levied at 17.5 per cent on the net cost of sales totalling £12,000. Will the tax be more than £2,000?

Answer

31 What is 324 divided by 12?

Answer

32 If tax is levied at 17.5 per cent, is it correct that £262,500 of tax would be payable on sales of one-and-a-half million pounds?

Answer

33 The instructions on a bottle recommend that you mix the contents with water at a ratio of 1:5 (ie five times as much water). How much water should you add to 225 ml of the bottle's contents?

Answer

34 If a train left at 11.35 am on a journey that normally takes 3 hours 20 minutes, but arrived 30 minutes late, what was its eventual time of arrival?

Answer

35 If the sterling/euro exchange rate is 1:1.53, how many euros would you receive in exchange for £20?

Answer

36 If an apartment in Venice was sold for 500,000 euros, would the vendor receive more or less than £320,000 if the sterling/euro exchange rate was 1:1.53?

Answer

37 By how many would the pig population grow if a sow was to have a litter of nine, and each of her offspring was to grow up and also have a first litter of nine?

Answer

38 In 2002 there were 530 secondary schools in Greater London. The government wanted to increase this total by 16 schools. What approximate percentage increase does this represent?

Answer

Quantitative reasoning

Attempt these questions without a calculator. Indicate your answer by writing the letter of the correct answer, A, B, C, D, E or F, in the answer box. Practise until you are able to answer each in under 30 seconds. Twenty-nine examples are given:

1   If a dozen pens cost £1.20, how much do three-and-a-half dozen cost?

A. £3.20	B. £32	C. £4.20
D. £2.20	E. £2.40	F. £3.10

Answer

2   Two identical parcels weigh 0.5 kg. One parcel and a letter weigh 0.35 kg. How much do two letters weigh?

A. 0.25 kg	B. 0.1 kg	C. 0.15 kg
D. 0.2 kg	E. 0.3 kg	F. 0.5 kg

Answer

3   A company took advantage of a special offer and bought an overhead pro-jector for one-third of its full price. How much was the discount?

A. 25%	B. 66.66%	C. 60%
D. 33.33%	E. 30%	F. 20%

Answer

4   In 2000, a company made a profit of £24,840. In 2001 the profit increased by one-quarter. How much profit did the company make in 2001?

A. £6,210	B. £30,050	C. £5,210
D. £32,050	E. £32,240	F. £31,050

Answer

5   In March Rob made 64 calls from his mobile, and his bill for March was £16. In April Rob made 25 per cent fewer calls. How many calls did Rob make in April, and how much was his bill?

A. 16 / £4	B. 48 / £12	C. 38 / £12
D. 32 / £12	E. 32 / £6	F. 34 / £4

Answer

6 The total business revenue for 2000 was £277,000. Staff wages were £67,000, overheads were £21,000 and production cost was £103,000. How much profit did the company make in 2000?

A. £262,000   B. £87,000   C. £98,000

D. £86,000   E. £96,000   F. £106,000

Answer [   ]

7 Mary is organizing transport for 150 conference attendees. If three coaches can accommodate 75 passengers, how many coaches should Mary hire?

A. 3   B. 2   C. 4

D. 6   E. 5   F. 7

Answer [   ]

8 The total amount of money generated by ticket sales for a conference is £1,134.00. The conference hall can accommodate 126 people. Assuming they all bought a ticket and paid the same price, what was the price of a single ticket?

A. £9   B. £11   C. £9.50

D. £10.50   E. £7   F. £8.50

Answer [   ]

9 Sophie works Monday to Friday. She leaves her house at 6.15 am to arrive at work at 7.45 am. It takes her just as long to get back home in the evening. How much time does she spend commuting per week?

A. 13 hours   B. 14.15 hours   C. 7.30 hours

D. 15 hours   E. 5 hours   F. 15.30 hours

Answer [   ]

10 Last week Ann worked 2 h overtime, Fred worked 1.30 h overtime, Lisa worked 1 h overtime, Mary worked 2.30 h overtime and Bob worked 3 h overtime. How many hours overtime did they work on average?

A. 10 hours   B. 3 hours   C. 2.32 hours

D. 2.30 hours   E. 2 hours   F. 3.32 hours

Answer [   ]

11 Phil is earning £70 per week and his wife Rose £80 per week. Phil receives a 5 per cent pay rise and Rose decides to work only part time, so she is earning 45 per cent less than before. How much is their new combined income per week?

A. £109.50   B. £108.10   C. £116.10

D. £117.50   E. £110.00   F. £197.50

Answer

12 A petty-cash box contains 7 × 50p coins, 18 × 20p coins, 33 × 10p coins, 12 × 5p coins and 15 × 2p coins. How much money in total is in the petty-cash box?

A. £23.10   B. £20.10   C. £21.10

D. £12.30   E. £15.30   F. £11.30

Answer

13 Twenty-four per cent of the staff working for a company are self-employed; the remainder are employed directly by the company. Of those directly employed, 18 per cent of the total staff work full time, while 29 members of staff are employed on a part-time basis. How many members of staff are self-employed?

A. 36   B. 29   C. 48

D. 18   E. 9   F. 12

Answer

14 The total capital invested into a partnership is £70,000. Partner A invested 2.5 times more than partner B. How much money did partner B invest?

A. £25,000   B. £50,000   C. £28,000

D. £20,000   E. £9,800   F. £19,800

Answer

15 If one photocopier can produce 180 copies per hour, how many copies can two photocopiers produce in 25 minutes?

A. 125   B. 175   C. 150

D. 145   E. 75   F. 200

Answer

16 Angela spends 7 hours per day in the office and works five days per week. She spends 3/7 of her time typing letters. How much time does Angela spend typing letters per week?

A. 15 hours   B. 7.30 hours   C. 20 hours

D. 20.30 hours   E. 15.30 hours   F. 12 hours

Answer

17 A carpet-cleaning company charges £2.25 per sq m. How much would it cost to clean a wall-to-wall carpet in an office sized 12 m by 18.5 m?

A. £222   B. £202   C. £499.50

D. £555   E. £495   F. £495.50

Answer

18 Hasan earns £400 per week before tax. His tax is £64 per week. In percentage terms, how much tax is Hasan paying?

A. 25%   B. 64%   C. 17.5%

D. 8%   E. 12%   F. 16%

Answer

19 An architect constructed a model of a shopping centre using a scale 1:2,000. If the model is 57.5 cm long, how long will the actual shopping centre be when built?

A. 11,500 m   B. 1,250 m   C. 115 m

D. 1,150 m   E. 115,000.00 m   F. 125 m

Answer

20 In an office, the ratio of male to female workers is 1:3.5. If there are four male workers, how many females work in the office?

A. 10   B. 12   C. 14

D. 8   E. 18   F. 13

Answer

21 Mojisola is taking a business trip to Italy. If the exchange rate for pounds sterling to euros is 1:1.6, and she needs 400 euros per day, how many pounds should she exchange for a four-day stay?

A. £857   B. £750   C. £849.50

D. £1,000   E. £600   F. £500

Answer

22 John earns £18,700 pa. Sarah earns £28,000 pa. How much is Mark earning pa if he earns 47 per cent less than John and Sarah together?

A. £24,751   B. £20,959   C. £18,959

D. £21,959   E. £21,949   F. £22,949

Answer

23   The profit for 1999 was £1,250. If the profit increases by 10 per cent each year, how much profit will be made in 2001?

A. £1,500   B. £1,512.50   C. £1,650

D. £1,525   E. £15,125   F. £1,652

Answer [   ]

24   The population in an area has a ratio of 3:7 young to old inhabitants. If a company wishes to reflect the same ratio among its 370 employees, how many of them should be old?

A. 259   B. 111   C. 255

D. 198   E. 220   F. 225

Answer [   ]

25   To reach its annual target, a sales team has to achieve on average 150 sales per quarter. At the end of the third quarter the sales are averaging 137 per quarter. How many sales must the sales team achieve during the final quarter to reach the target?

A. 211   B. 123   C. 189

D. 150   E. 137   F. 411

Answer [   ]

26   Susan earns £15,400 pa after paying 23 per cent tax. How much is her annual income before tax?

A. £20,000   B. £17,220   C. £24,780

D. £15,376   E. £16,450   F. £18,881

Answer [   ]

27   Company A employs twice as many people as Company B. Company C employs 25 per cent fewer people than Company A. If Company C employs 120, how many does Company B employ?

A. 75   B. 60   C. 150

D. 120   E. 80   F. 160

Answer [   ]

28   The size of an office is 11 m by 12.5 m. How many carpet tiles sized 50 cm by 50 cm are required to cover the office floor, excluding the area underneath the filing cabinet? The base of the filing cabinet is 1.25 m by 80 cm.

A. 568	B. 546	C. 548
D. 136.5	E. 188	F. 176.5

Answer ▢

29 The budget for organizing a seminar is £3,700. Of this, 35 per cent is spent on hiring a venue. A quarter of the remainder is used to pay a speaker, while 2/3 is paid for transport to and from the venue. How much of the budget is left for refreshments? Round your answer to the nearest pound.

A. £199	B. £217	C. £170
D. £153	E. £200	F. £76

Answer ▢

Data interpretation

This type of test comprises tables or charts of information that you must interpret in order to answer the questions that follow. Thirty-four examples are provided. Indicate your answer by writing the letter of the correct answer, A, B, C, D, E or F, in the answer box.

TABLE 2.1 Acceptances for settlement in the UK: by category of acceptance

	Thousands			
	1985	1990	1995	2000
New Commonwealth				
Own right	4.1	2.4	1.7	1.6
Husbands	3.2	3.2	6.3	6.0
Wives	10.0	3.9	9.6	9.6
Children	10.7	3.2	4.5	4.5
Others	3.4	3.3	5.8	6.1
Total New Commonwealth	31.4	16.0	27.9	27.8
Rest of the world				
Own right	11.6	6.6	9.3	4.0
Husbands	3.4	6.1	5.4	4.9
Wives	6.8	4.8	3.7	9.0
Children	3.7	2.9	3.1	3.9
Others	2.3	3.6	4.7	3.2
Total rest of the world	27.8	24.0	26.2	25.0
Total acceptances	59.2	40.0	54.1	52.8

1   How many people settled in the UK in 2000?

A. 25,000   B. 27,000   C. 48,000

D. 52,600   E. 54,000   F. 59,200

Answer [   ]

2   In which year were acceptances from the New Commonwealth proportionally less than from the rest of the world?

A. 1985   B. 1990   C. 1995

D. 2000   E. none   F. information not available

Answer [   ]

3   In 1995 which category was the least accepted overall?

A. own right   B. husbands   C. wives

D. children   E. others   F. none

Answer [   ]

4   How many more children from the rest of the world were accepted in 2000 than in 1985?

A. 0   B. 20   C. 200

D. 800   E. 2,000   F. 8,000

Answer [   ]

5   What percentage of total acceptances in 1990 were from the New Commonwealth?

A. 20%   B. 40%   C. 60%

D. 70%   E. 80%   F. 90%

Answer [   ]

TABLE 2.2 All aboard the ferry: summer 2002 timetable*

Pier Head depart	Seaway arrive/depart	Riverside arrive/depart	Pier Head arrive	Fare (£)
10.00 am	10.30 am	10.40 am	10.50 am	2.20
11.00 am	11.30 am	11.40 am	11.50 am	2.20
12.00 pm	12.30 pm	12.40 pm	12.50 pm	2.20
1.00 pm	1.30 pm	1.40 pm	1.50 pm	2.20
2.00 pm	2.30 pm	2.40 pm	2.50 pm	2.20
3.00 pm	3.30 pm	3.40 pm	3.50 pm	2.20
4.15 pm	4.25 pm	4.35 pm	4.45 pm	1.15
4.45 pm	4.55 pm	5.05 pm	5.15 pm	1.15
5.15 pm	5.25 pm	5.35 pm	5.45 pm	1.15
5.45 pm	5.55 pm	6.05 pm	6.15 pm	1.15

* Between 10.00 am and 3.00 pm the ferry makes a scenic round trip, leaving Pier Head each hour on the hour.

6 How long is the scenic cruise?

A. 30 minutes   B. 50 minutes   C. 1 hour

D. 5 hours   E. 6 hours   F. 6 hours 15 minutes
   50 minutes

Answer _____

7 What time does the 1.00 pm ferry from Pier Head arrive at Riverside?

A. 1.30 pm   B. 1.40 pm   C. 1.50 pm

D. 2.00 pm   E. 2.40 pm   F. 3.00 pm

Answer _____

8 What is the longest time the ferry waits at Pier Head?

A. 5 minutes   B. 10 minutes   C. 15 minutes

D. 20 minutes   E. 25 minutes   F. 30 minutes

Answer _____

9 A party of 50 tourists board the 2.00 pm scenic cruise. How much in total do they pay for this tour?

A. £57.50   B. £65.00   C. £100.00

D. £110.00   E. £125.00   F. £140.00

Answer _____

10   At 4.00 pm a tanker anchors off Seaway. This results in a 15-minute delay between Seaway and Riverside on all journeys from then on. What time does the ferry finally finish at Pier Head that day?

A. 5.00 pm   B. 5.15 pm   C. 6.15 pm

D. 6.45 pm   E. 7.15 pm   F. insufficient information

Answer [   ]

Delilah Smythe is baking cakes, but she has a gas oven and the recipe only gives temperatures in °C. She therefore looks up her handy conversion table.

TABLE 2.3 Conversion table

| | Oven temperatures | |
Gas mark	°F	°C
1	275	140
2	300	150
3	325	170
4	350	180
5	375	190
6	400	200
7	425	220
8	450	230
9	475	240

11   The recipe says 'Bake the cakes at 180°C for 20–25 minutes until brown on top.' What gas mark should Delilah use?

A. 1   B. 2   C. 3   D. 4   E. 5   F. 6

Answer [   ]

12   At gas marks 2 and 6, what is the difference between the readings in °F and °C?

A. ×1   B. ×2   C. ×3   D. ×4   E. ×5   F. ×6

Answer [   ]

13   What is the range in temperature, measured in °F, between gas marks 3 and 9?

A. 70°F   B. 100°F   C. 125°F

D. 150°F   E. 175°F   F. 200°F

Answer [   ]

14   Delilah uses a thermometer to check the temperature of her oven at the various gas marks and finds that gas mark 6 is 5 per cent higher than it should be. What temperature, in °C, does the thermometer read?

A. 190° C   B. 200°C   C. 210°C

D. 220°C   E. 230°C   F. 240°C

Answer [   ]

The Stephenson family love to shop. The family of five easily spends over £300 each week at Sainsway's on groceries. Here is part of their till receipt for one week in March:

CUCUMBER WHOLE	0.59	g
ORGANIC ORANGES	1.49	g
S GREENS	0.75	g
S P/NUT/BUT SMTH	1.99	
S P/NUT/BUT SMTH	1.99	
MULTISAVE	−1.99	
S SATSUMA LARGE	1.79	g
PURE ORANGE JUICEX1LTR	0.99	
S SOAP MULTIPACK	1.75	
S SATSUMA LARGE	1.79	g
MULTISAVE	−1.79	
S TOOTHPASTE	0.88	
0.745 kg @ £2.49 / kg		
S GRAPES WHT S/LESS	1.86	g
**** TOT	302.60	
16/03/02 16.07		

FIGURE 2.1 Till receipt

15   How much is one litre of pure orange juice?

A. £0.99   B. £1.49   C. £1.75

D. £1.79   E. £1.99   F. information not supplied

Answer [   ]

16   How much have the Stephenson family saved on multisaves?

A. £1.79   B. £1.99   C. £2.67

D. £3.78   E. £4.02   F. £4.52

Answer [   ]

17   How much did the Stephenson family spend on groceries (g)?

A. £0.56   B. £1.42   C. £3.65

D. £5.64   E. £6.48   F. £8.27

Answer [   ]

18   Mrs Stephenson has collected 250 discount points on her loyalty card, worth 10 per cent of the total bill. How much does she save?

A. £20.50   B. £25.00   C. £30.26

D. £33.60   E. £40.62   F. £40.88

Answer [   ]

TABLE 2.4 Holiday entitlement

Name	Annual holiday entitlement	Carry-over from the previous year	Total numbers of days taken to date	Days remaining
M Adams	23	0	1.5	21.5
S Brown	23	−1	11	?
H Evans	27	2	5	?
H Hasan	26	0	5	?
A Milic	23	−1.5	8	?

19   From Table 2.4, how many more days' holiday can S Brown take in the current year?

A. 22   B. 24   C. 11   D. 21   E. 19   F. 18

Answer [   ]

20   Employees are given 23 days' holiday per year during the first two years of service and then an extra half day for every six months of service. How many years has H Hasan been with the company?

A. 4   B. 6   C. 4.5   D. 5   E. 3.5   F. 5.5

Answer [   ]

21   A Milic earns £300 per week. If she decides to resign and work throughout her notice period without taking any more holiday, how much holiday pay will she be entitled to? Assume that her last day of employment coincides with the end of the year for holiday entitlement purposes.

A. £900   B. £22.22   C. £810

D. £620   E. £720   F. £600

Answer

22   If S Brown wants to go away for 15 days, how many days' unpaid leave should he take in addition to his holiday entitlement?

A. 5   B. 3   C. 0

D. 1   E. 4   F. 2

Answer

Table 2.5 shows the realized sales of a mobile phone package priced at £49, and the commission earned per sale.

TABLE 2.5 Mobile phone package sales

Name	Target in units	Units sold	Commission (%)	Total (%)	Earnings
S Amed	25	24	3	35.28	
B Fay	25	31	3	?	
S Grant	25	28	3	41.16	
I Jones	25	21	3	30.87	
O Khann	25	26	3	38.22	
A Lewis	25	26	3	38.22	

23   From the table, calculate the total commission earned by B Fay.

A. £28.30   B. £93.00   C. £45.57

D. £36.75   E. £55.75   F. £28.00

Answer

24   On average, how many units did each salesperson sell during the period?

A. 26   B. 22   C. 21

D. 29   E. 27   F. 28

Answer

25 If the company decided to increase the commission to 5 per cent for every unit sold above the target, how much commission would S Grant earn?

A. £52.30   B. £60   C. £37.75

D. £53.17   E. £44.10   F. £43.17

Answer [   ]

26 What percentage of employees reached the target?

A. 25%   B. 30%   C. 60%

D. 70%   E. 66.6%   F. 33.3%

Answer [   ]

Table 2.6 shows the net total (income after tax) generated by the products.

TABLE 2.6 Net total generated by products

Product	Number of units (in 000s)	Cost of raw material per unit (£)	Manufacturing cost per unit (£)	Total cost per unit (£)	Sales price per unit (£)	Total sales revenue (£) (sales price – total cost × number of units)
a	21.5	3.75	2	5.75	7.5	37,625.00
b	18	2.19	3.17	5.36	6.25	1,602.00
c	7	8.70	4.2	12.90	13.4	3,500.00
d	11.75	0.57	4.8	5.37	7.99	?
e	12.8	1.18	0.27	1.45	4.5	39,040.00
f	9.25	4.3	1.5	5.8	6.25	4,162.50
Total	80.3	20.69	15.94	36.63	45.89	743,578.00
Profit (−23%)					?	

27 From the table, calculate which product is the most profitable.

A. f   B. d   C. e   D. a   E. c   F. b

Answer [   ]

28 If the manufacturing cost were reduced by 50 per cent, what would be the total sales revenue for product a?

A. £60,700   B. £49,125   C. £57,755

D. £59,125   E. £48,950   F. £66,789

Answer [   ]

29 Calculate the total sales revenue for product d.

A. £40,500   B. £30,785   C. £30,885

D. £45,125   E. £33,600   F. £30,780

Answer [   ]

30 Assuming that the tax is 23 per cent, calculate the total profit for the period.

A. £572,555.06   B. £57,255.56   C. £171,022.94

D. £17,122.94   E. £743,250.00   F. £74,325.00

Answer [   ]

TABLE 2.7 Average temperatures in °C

Year	1st quarter	2nd quarter	3rd quarter	4th quarter
1996	1	12.5	23	2
1997	2	11	22	4
1998	−1	13.5	24	3.5
1999	0	10	21.5	4
2000	1.5	15.5	23	2
2001	2	14.5	25	?

31 From Table 2.7, what was the average temperature in 1999?

A. 8.9°C   B. 9°C   C. 8.8°C

D. 11.8°C   E. 11.7°C   F. 10.7°C

Answer [   ]

32 Calculate the net change in temperature between the first and fourth quarters for 1998.

A. 2.25°C   B. 4.5°C   C. 3.5°C

D. 2.5°C   E. −4°C   F. −4.5°C

Answer [   ]

33 In what year was the greatest change in temperature between the first and third quarters?

A. 1996   B. 1997   C. 1998

D. 1999   E. 2000   F. 2001

Answer [   ]

34 If the average temperature in 2000 was the same as in 2001, what was the temperature in the final quarter in 2001?

A. 2   B. 2.5   C. 1.5

D. 1   E. 5   F. 0.5

Answer [   ]

Word swap

Each question comprises a sentence in which two words need to be interchanged to make it read sensibly. Swap only two words, so that one replaces the other. This means that one word must be placed where you have taken the other. Try the following 19 examples:

1 A loss of muscle movement is accompanied by rapid tone of the eyes.

Answer [   ]

2 Sometimes these remedies can result remarkably quickly, with a positive work occurring in a matter of hours.

Answer [   ]

3 Completely safe, it is made from artificial ingredients, with no natural colours, flavours or preservatives.

Answer [   ]

4 Over the centuries and of these properties have been sold some other properties purchased.

Answer [   ]

5 Only the small doorway in the remain on the ground floor and a similar doorway on the northern wall of the gallery recess today.

Answer [   ]

6 They take most day as it comes and work very hard to make the each of it.

Answer [   ]

7   Perhaps the greatest advantage to the constant ability is see two sides to every story.

Answer [   ]

8   It's true they have an enthusiastic style for information and a bubbly hunger of expression.

Answer [   ]

9   The national minimum wage is over £4.20 an hour for workers aged 22 years or now.

Answer [   ]

10   How thrilling to camp out in the jungle surrounded of the incredible sounds by the equatorial night.

Answer [   ]

11   Many people believe that we should eat our national produce more and only respect fruit and vegetables that are in season.

Answer [   ]

12   If your dog does kill a rabbit it may be necessary for you to put the rabbit out of its misery and catch it yourself.

Answer [   ]

13   A few golfers rake to forget the sand in the bunker after their shot, which can cause problems for the next person.

Answer [   ]

14   The most popular numerous orange is the Seville, a thin-skinned orange-red fruit, with acid, deep yellow flesh and bitter pips.

Answer [   ]

15   The adaptable alphabet is the most highly developed, convenient and the most easily Roman system of writing.

Answer [   ]

16   A damp-proof course is a layer of inserted material impervious in the bottom of a house wall about 20 cm above ground level.

Answer [   ]

17   There are few things as idyllic as opening up the picnic basket in an irritating spot only to find the tin/bottle opener is back on the kitchen table.

Answer [   ]

18   The known benefits of raw fish, soya beans and green tea have long been health to the Japanese.

Answer [   ]

19   It would be unwise to venture out of the house during springtime in England about an umbrella without one's person.

Answer [   ]

Missing words

In each of the sentences below, two words are missing. Beneath the sentence are four groups of two words each. One group has the two words in the order in which they fall in the sentence. It is your task to identify which are the correct pairings from the sound-alike or look-alike alternatives.

Indicate your answer by writing the letters of the correct pair, A, B, C or D, in the answer box. Try the following 21 examples:

1   To .... any sort of change, the proposed legislation must have an .... that is clearly felt by the community.

A	B	C	D
affect	effect	aphect	ephect
effect	effect	ephect	aphect

Answer [   ]

2   He was .... upon the goodwill of his father; he was after all his sole
....

A	B	C	D
depandent	dependant	dependent	deapendent
depandant	dependent	dependant	deapandant

Answer [   ]

3   He .... with pleasure his .... to fish in the Loch.

A	B	C	D
excepted	accepted	excepted	accepted
license	licence	licence	license

Answer [   ]

4 It will be on David's .... if Lucy does not remain .... throughout the night.

A	B	C	D
concience	conscience	conscience	concience
conscious	conscious	consious	consious

Answer [   ]

5 The girl .... a glass out of the .... window.

A	B	C	D
threw	through	threw	though
rear	rare	reer	wrear

Answer [   ]

6 The cutter he was going to use to .... the tree had a blueish .... to it.

A	B	C	D
hugh	hew	hue	huw
hue	hue	hew	hugh

Answer [   ]

7 Honesty was Helen's first .... when she became .... of the school.

A	B	C	D
princepal	principle	principle	principal
princaple	principle	principal	principal

Answer [   ]

8 It is common .... to .... to the queen as she passes.

A	B	C	D
courtesy	curtesy	courtesey	curtesey
curtsy	quertsey	courtsey	qurtsey

Answer [   ]

9   The raid on the .... resulted in .... action being taken.

A	B	C	D
dispensery	dispensary	disspensary	disspensery
disciplinery	disciplinary	disiplinary	disiplinery

Answer [   ]

10   She kept a .... of artefacts for when the .... of pilgrims came by.

A	B	C	D
horde	hord	hoard	whord
hoarde	herd	horde	wherd

Answer [   ]

11   What you can do to make your cut .... last even longer is to dip the cut
ends in .... before putting them in water.

A	B	C	D
flours	fluers	flowers	flouers
flower	flouer	flour	fluer

Answer [   ]

12   Take a .... of fruit and .... the skin with a pin.

A	B	C	D
peice	piece	peace	piece
pearce	peirce	peirse	pierce

Answer [   ]

13   I had to .... the authorities she was too .... to travel.

A	B	C	D
informe	inform	infourm	informn
inferm	infirm	inferme	infirmn

Answer [   ]

14 It was the .... of such a musician to .... for five hours each day.

A	B	C	D
practise	practice	practisce	practicse
practice	practise	practicse	practisce

Answer [　　　　　]

15 It was while the van was .... at the traffic lights that the .... on board was stolen.

A	B	C	D
stationary	stationery	stationray	stationarey
stationery	stationary	stationrey	stationeray

Answer [　　　　　]

16 On the back of the .... was a .... for marmalade.

A	B	C	D
rescite	resept	reciept	receipt
resepy	recipy	receipe	recipe

Answer [　　　　　]

17 For the best results you must do the .... upon getting up.

A	B	C	D
excersises	exersises	excercises	exercises
imediately	immidiately	immedietely	immediately

Answer [　　　　　]

18 As a .... you are not allowed to .... the machine.

A	B	C	D
miner	minor	miener	mienor
opporate	operate	oparate	operate

Answer [　　　　　]

19 These .... took those other .... books by mistake.

A	B	C	D
boys	bouys	boy's	boys'
boys'	bouy's	boys	boy's

Answer [   ]

20 .... most unusual for the dog to refuse .... bone like that.

A	B	C	D
Its	It's	Its'	It
it's	its	it	its'

Answer [   ]

21 Even when using a .... line the wall does not look ....

A	B	C	D
plum	plumb	plump	plumn
strait	straight	strate	streight

Answer [   ]

Correct sentences

Identify which of the options is correct in terms of grammar, spelling and punctuation. Below you will find 20 examples of this type of question. Indicate your answer by writing the letter of the correct sentence, A, B, C or D, in the answer box.

1 A. If you're looking for an evening out this month, there are big offers on musicals and pop concerts.

   B. If you're looking for an evening out this month, there is big offers on musicals and pop concerts.

   C. If your looking for an evening out this month, there are big offers on musicals and pop concerts.

   D. None of these.

Answer [   ]

2   A. The consumer is protected from exploitation by a given seller by the exist-
         ence of other seller's he can buy from.

     B. The consumer is protected from exploitation by a given seller by the exist-
         ence of other sellers from whom he can buy.

     C. The consumer are protected from exploitation by a given seller by the exist-
         ence of other sellers from whom he can buy.

     D. None of these.

                                                        Answer [   ]

3   A. All mammal's produce eggs within which their young develop.

     B. All mammal's produce eggs which their young develop in.

     C. All mammals produce eggs within which their young develop.

     D. None of these.

                                                        Answer [   ]

4   A. There are maps and travel books available for most of England's towns and
         cities.

     B. There is maps and travel books available for most of England's towns and
         cities.

     C. Maps and travel books is available for most of England's Towns and Cities.

     D. None of these.

                                                        Answer [   ]

5   A. Further information will be given to you when you visited the head office.

     B. Further information was given to you when you visit the head office.

     C. Further information will be given to you when you visit the head office.

     D. None of these.

                                                        Answer [   ]

6   A. She married again, which surprised everybody who knew her.

     B. She married again, what surprised everybody who knew her.

     C. She married again, that surprised everybody whom knew her.

     D. None of these.

                                                        Answer [   ]

7   A. There are a wide selection of gifts available, all of which can be ordered by post or online.

    B. There is a wide selection of gifts available, all of which can be ordered by post or online.

    C. There is a wide selection of gifts available, all of which will be ordered by post or online.

    D. None of these.

Answer
_____

8   A. At that moment, I wished I had gone to the same university as John.

    B. At that moment, I wished I was gone to the same university as John.

    C. At that moment, I wished I had gone to the same university as John did.

    D. None of these.

Answer
_____

9   A. When I go to university I'll not have no time for reading novels.

    B. When I go to university I won't have no time for reading novels.

    C. When I go to university I will have no time for reading novels.

    D. None of these.

Answer
_____

10   A. The coach was expecting great things off the team this season.

    B. The coach was expecting great things of the team this season.

    C. The coach were expecting great things of the team this season.

    D. None of these.

Answer
_____

11   A. Whenever a new book comes out she is the first to buy a copy.

    B. Whenever a new book comes out she are the first to buy a copy.

    C. Whenever a new book comes out she is the first too buy a copy.

    D. None of these.

Answer
_____

12   A. There are the promise of a more secure future for those who save on a regular basis.

    B. There is the promise of a more secure future for those who save on a regular basis.

C. Their is the promise of a more secure future for those who saved on a regular basis.

D. None of these.

Answer [   ]

13 A. If the customer does return the goods, you must check them before you gave a refund.

B. If the customer did return the goods, you must ensure you check them before giving a refund.

C. If the customer should return the goods, you must ensure you check them before giving a refund.

D. None of the above.

Answer [   ]

14 A. There's places where that kind of behaviour is unacceptable.

B. There are places where that kind of behaviour is unacceptable.

C. There's place's where that kind of behaviour is unacceptable.

D. None of these.

Answer [   ]

15 A. This borough is very good about providing bins for recycling metal, plastic, glass and paper.

B. This borough are very good about providing bins for recycling metal, plastic, glass and paper.

C. This borough is very good while providing bins for recycling metal, plastic, glass and paper.

D. None of these.

Answer [   ]

16 A. One of the most important notes on the piano are Middle C.

B. One of the most important note's on the piano is Middle C.

C. One of the most important notes on the piano is Middle C.

D. None of these.

Answer [   ]

17 A. Once Simon got angry it takes a long while for him to calm down.

B. Once Simon gets angry it takes a long while for him to calm down.

C. Once Simon gets angry it took a long while for him to calm down.

D. None of these.

Answer [   ]

18 A. We pitched our tent on the bank of the river Stour, near where it joins the Avon.

B. We pitched our tent on the bank of the river Stour, near where it joined the Avon.

C. We pitched our tent on the bank of the river Stour, near where it is joining the Avon.

D. None of these.

Answer [   ]

19 A. They was walking along the beach all day yesterday and they will be walking along the cliff all day tomorrow.

B. They were walking along the beach all day yesterday and they were walking along the cliff all day tomorrow.

C. They were walking along the beach all day yesterday and they will be walking along the cliff all day tomorrow.

D. None of these.

Answer [   ]

20 A. It was Galileo who discovered that Jupiter has moons.

B. It was Galileo whom discovered that Jupiter had moons.

C. It's Galileo who discovered that Jupiter had moons.

D. None of these.

Answer [   ]

Following procedures

This exercise measures your ability to follow explicit rules and interpret given information.

You are presented with a choice of 10 possible answers from which you must select the correct one(s). Please note that some of the practice questions require more than one suggested answer to be marked as correct. Indicate your answer by writing the letter(s) of the correct answer(s), A–J, in the answer box.

A credit management process

The flow chart in Figure 2.2 illustrates the key points of the process.

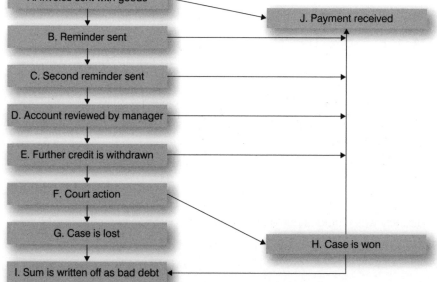

FIGURE 2.2 Credit management flow chart

Rules governing the credit process

1 Invoices are sent out with goods and state that the company operates a strict 20-day credit facility from the date of invoice.
2 The first reminder is sent out 14 days after the goods. If payment is still not received, the second reminder is sent after a further 10 days.
3 Account reviews are held 17 days after the issuing of the second reminder.
4 In cases when the sum owed exceeds £100 and payment is not received within 20 days from the date of the account review, court action is instigated.
5 If the court case is lost, the amount is written off as a bad debt.
6 Without exception, credit facilities are withdrawn when the court action is initiated or when any sum becomes more than 60 days overdue.

1   Payment was received 22 working days after the date of invoice. What stage of the credit process would have last been implemented?

   A   B   C   D   E   F   G   H   I   J

                                        Answer [   ]

2   Court action has had to be initiated against a creditor. What would have been the action taken immediately prior to this?

A   B   C   D   E   F   G   H   I   J

Answer [   ]

3   A creditor has owed £98 for almost two months. What action should be taken?

A   B   C   D   E   F   G   H   I   J

Answer [   ]

4   The average time taken for payment to be received is 39 working days from the invoice date. What stage of the process would next be initiated if payment was not received by then?

A   B   C   D   E   F   G   H   I   J

Answer [   ]

5   Identify which stages could precede a debt being written off as bad.

A   B   C   D   E   F   G   H   I   J

Answer [   ]

6   A payment has still not been received after 30 days. What action could be taken?

A   B   C   D   E   F   G   H   I   J

Answer [   ]

7   What are the possible outcomes from court action?

A   B   C   D   E   F   G   H   I   J

Answer [   ]

8   Twenty days have passed since a case review. The sum outstanding is £120. What action should be taken?

A   B   C   D   E   F   G   H   I   J

Answer [   ]

9   What actions can an account manager recommend?

A   B   C   D   E   F   G   H   I   J

Answer [   ]

10 Since the date of the invoice, 41 days have passed. What action is due to be taken?

A   B   C   D   E   F   G   H   I   J

Answer [   ]

Speed and accuracy

The following speed and accuracy questions require you to compare sets of numbers or letters arranged in pairs, one on the left, the other on the right. Each set consists of four pairs, and you have to indicate how many of them are identical. You are offered five possible answers: all four (are identical), three pairs, two pairs, one pair or none. Indicate your answer by writing the letter of the correct answer, A, B, C, D or E, in the answer box.

1   45981   45981
        xsbaa   xssa
        kiyhq   kiyhq
        21213   21213

A. all 4   B. 3 pairs   C. 2 pairs   D. 1 pair   E. none

Answer [   ]

2   qwdfk   wqdfk
        33601   33611
        15380   15580
        50179   97150

A. all 4   B. 3 pairs   C. 2 pairs   D. 1 pair   E. none

Answer [   ]

3   hjwep   hjwep
        ffthm   ftthm
        abelo   abelo
        mwwgr   mnwgr

A. all 4   B. 3 pairs   C. 2 pairs   D. 1 pair   E. none

Answer [   ]

4
58392	53892
dmhmi	dmdmi
bdbdv	dbdbv
illia	ilila

A. all 4   B. 3 pairs   C. 2 pairs   D. 1 pair   E. none

Answer

5
zxasw	zxasw
74893	74893
17204	12704
01010	01020

A. all 4   B. 3 pairs   C. 2 pairs   D. 1 pair   E. none

Answer

6
bgdth	gbdth
zakiv	zakii
45000	54001
45001	45000

A. all 4   B. 3 pairs   C. 2 pairs   D. 1 pair   E. none

Answer

7
sopme	soome
soppq	soppq
04517	04518
49872	49872

A. all 4   B. 3 pairs   C. 2 pairs   D. 1 pair   E. none

Answer

8
mmhhi	mmhhh
99933	33399
fffrr	ffrr
nhqir	nhqir

A. all 4   B. 3 pairs   C. 2 pairs   D. 1 pair   E. none

Answer

9   nxruy   nxruy
       qqasw   qqasw
       93462   93462
       ntyue   nteyu

A. all 4   B. 3 pairs   C. 2 pairs   D. 1 pair   E. none

Answer _____

10 15795   15795
       48957   48957
       25846   25864
       35745   35754

A. all 4   B. 3 pairs   C. 2 pairs   D. 1 pair   E. none

Answer _____

11 ilop   kliop
       kopli   kploi
       poilk   polik
       oolip   ollip

A. all 4   B. 3 pairs   C. 2 pairs   D. 1 pair   E. none

Answer _____

12 vfrtg   fgtrv
       gfrtv   gfrtv
       frtgv   frtgv
       gfrtf   rtfgt

A. all 4   B. 3 pairs   C. 2 pairs   D. 1 pair   E. none

Answer _____

13 20250   25052
       0425   0425
       65658   65658
       20052   20052

A. all 4   B. 3 pairs   C. 2 pairs   D. 1 pair   E. none

Answer _____

14   blgos   blgos
      werqw   werqw
      14584   14584
      36526   36526

      A. all 4   B. 3 pairs   C. 2 pairs   D. 1 pair   E. none

Answer

15   07078   07078
      asdfg   asdfg
      gfdsa   gfdsa
      03256   03256

      A. all 4   B. 3 pairs   C. 2 pairs   D. 1 pair   E. none

Answer

16   wuyoi   wuyoi
      30057   30057
      dflkk   dflkk
      45008   45008

      A. all 4   B. 3 pairs   C. 2 pairs   D. 1 pair   E. none

Answer

17   49057   49057
      00558   00558
      asiore   asoire
      nheppo   nheppo

      A. all 4   B. 3 pairs   C. 2 pairs   D. 1 pair   E. none

Answer

18   4584584   4584584
      32658   32658
      500505   500505
      054585   0548458

      A. all 4   B. 3 pairs   C. 2 pairs   D. 1 pair   E. none

Answer

19   gpr ty   gprty
         druowff   druuowff
         foluaw   foluaw
         brtrt   brtrt

A. all 4   B. 3 pairs   C. 2 pairs   D. 1 pair   E. none

Answer [ ]

20   137946   137946
         438679   438679
         402794   4022794
         4586003   4586603

A. all 4   B. 3 pairs   C. 2 pairs   D. 1 pair   E. none

Answer [ ]

21   df er ty s   df er ty s
         fgtyoui   fgtyuoi
         cdf gtyg   cdfgtyy
         mmyyeeq   mmyyyeq

A. all 4   B. 3 pairs   C. 2 pairs   D. 1 pair   E. none

Answer [ ]

22   fdfre gt   fdre gg
         25 87 5   25 87 5
         bru ew   bru ee
         1579 587   1597 587

A. all 4   B. 3 pairs   C. 2 pairs   D. 1 pair   E. none

Answer [ ]

23   kuyjkrr   kuyjkrr
         qwqwreee   qwqwreeee
         nwkyiunn   nmkyiunn
         vetuyooi   vetyuooi

A. all 4   B. 3 pairs   C. 2 pairs   D. 1 pair   E. none

Answer [ ]

CHAPTER 3

Practice tests for the administrative grades

The questions in this chapter have been arranged as practice tests with recommended time limits. The tests are realistic in terms of the question types and, most importantly, in terms of the sheer hard work and extended concentration required to do well in them. Develop these skills and they will serve you well in every psychometric test you take.

Use this chapter to practise under realistic test-like conditions. You should aim to develop a winning exam technique and to improve the rate at which you can answer the questions while not making too many mistakes. With this sort of practice your confidence in your abilities will soon increase, as will your mental stamina and agility. Practise getting your time management right. Do not spend too long on any single question; if you really can't answer one, then use educated guessing. This involves looking at the suggested answers and trying to rule out some as wrong, then guessing from the remaining options. Use any time at the end to check your answers. Realize that doing well in a test is not only down to your intelligence but also requires you to try your very best. So really go for it.

After each test, review the answers and explanations provided. Pay particular attention to any questions that you got wrong. Then take the next test. To make the test seem even more realistic, stick strictly to the suggested time limit and work without interruption or disturbance.

Our minds are wonderful things but prone to be a bit lazy. We can so easily convince ourselves that we have learnt something when in fact we have not. The only way to tell if we really have mastered something is to test ourselves.

Practice test 1 Quantitative reasoning

This test consists of 30 questions. Allow yourself 20 minutes to complete it.

Set a stopwatch or the stopwatch function on a mobile phone, and stick strictly to the recommended time limit.

Be sure to revise your mental arithmetic before you sit a real test of quantitative reasoning. You may well be allowed to use a calculator in this type of test, so if you wish to use one in these practice tests, then do so, but sparingly. You still need to be sure of your mental arithmetic because then you will be better placed to see any error you might have made with the calculator. Moreover, you can often answer the questions faster if you do not have to check each calculation. Beware also if you are applying for lots of jobs, as you may well come up against a test in which a calculator is not allowed.

Select one answer from the suggested list. Indicate your answer by writing the letter of the correct answer in the answer box. Scrap paper is useful to help with any calculations.

Do not start until you are ready to begin. Keep going until you have completed the last question or run out of time.

Quantitative reasoning

1   A secretary is posting 11 letters to clients. She is sending seven letters by first-class post at 27p per letter. The remaining four letters she is sending by second-class post at 19p per letter. How much postage is being paid for all 11 letters?

A. £2.77   B. £1.27   C. £1.76

D. £2.41   E. £2.56   F. £2.65

Answer

2   A delivery was due to arrive at 14.45 but was 27 minutes late. At what time did it arrive?

A. 15.07   B. 15.05   C. 15.22

D. 15.12   E. 15.42   F. 15.02

Answer

3   Ann deposits £1,000.00 in her savings account. The interest rate on her savings is 5 per cent. How long is it before Ann has earned £157 of interest?

A. 2.5 years   B. 3.5 years   C. 4 years

D. 1.5 years   E. 1 year   F. 3 years

Answer

4   A company purchased a new PC for £800. The depreciation rate (decrease in value) is 40 per cent for the first year and 25 per cent of the depreciated sum for every following year. What is the value of the PC at the end of the third year?

A. £48   B. £240   C. £270

D. £280   E. £230   F. £58

Answer

5   An office junior can type 30 wpm. If he types steadily for 30 minutes, how many words will he type?

A. 90   B. 600   C. 60

D. 120   E. 800   F. 900

Answer

6 An accountant has worked for a company for four months. His holiday allowance is 1.25 days per month in service. How many holiday days is the accountant entitled to after four months' service?

A. 4.25 days   B. 6 days   C. 5.5 days

D. 3 days   E. 5 days   F. 2 days

                                                     Answer _____

7 Petra is ordering stationery. She orders two boxes of staples at £1.75 each and five large notebooks at £1.15 each. All these prices are shown before VAT (17.5 per cent). How much will the total be including VAT?

A. £10.45   B. £9.45   C. £9.75

D. £10.87   E. £11.75   F. £9.65

                                                     Answer _____

8 A company manufactures small, medium and large buttons at the ratio of 1:5:3. If in 2001 the total of buttons manufactured was 18,900, how many of them were large?

A. 2,100   B. 6,300   C. 10,500

D. 1,300   E. 13,600   F. 6,800

                                                     Answer _____

9 A parcel weighing 1 kg costs £3.50 to post. If prices are proportional to weight, how much would it cost to post a parcel that weighs 200 g?

A. £1.75   B. £1.25   C. £0.75

D. £0.70   E. £1.15   F. £0.89

                                                     Answer _____

10 A meeting is scheduled to start at 2:45 pm and last for 1 h 30 m. The trip from the office to the meeting venue takes 45 minutes. If Barbara is to attend the meeting, how long will she be away from the office?

A. 3 h   B. 2 h 45 m   C. 3 h 15 m

D. 4 h   E. 2 h 30 m   F. 3 h 45 m

                                                     Answer _____

11 A company decides to buy corporate membership for its employees at the local gym. The gym is offering 20 per cent discount on all corporate memberships. How many members of staff should join for the company to receive the equivalent of two free memberships?

A. 5   B. 12   C. 8

D. 10   E. 20   F. 15

Answer [   ]

12 With a buy-one-get-one-free offer, what percentage is saved?

A. 25%   B. 33%   C. 50%

D. 20%   E. 35%   .   F. 75%

Answer [   ]

13 The total postage cost for two parcels of different weight is £3.40. If the weight ratio is 2:2.3, calculate the postage for the heavier parcel.

A. £1.57   B. £2.10   C. £1.82

D. £1.90   E. £2.18   F. £2.40

Answer [   ]

14 Attendee A and attendee B are arriving for the same meeting from different locations. Attendee A is travelling at 47 mph over the distance of 38 miles. Attendee B is travelling at 38 mph over 29 miles. If they start their journeys at the same time, what will be the time gap between their arrivals? Round your answer up to a full minute.

A. 5 mins   B. 3 mins   C. 2 mins

D. 7 mins   E. 8 mins   F. 4 mins

Answer [   ]

15 If 3 per cent of the price is £24, how much is the full price?

A. £600   B. £240   C. £750

D. £850   E. £400   F. £800

Answer [   ]

16 A company is running a special promotion and is discounting its product by 25 per cent. If the price before the discount was £10 and the total revenue was £1,000, by what percentage should sales increase to generate the same amount of revenue as before the reduction?

A. 7.5%   B. 25%   C. 10%

D. 33.3%   E. 12.5%   F. 15%

Answer [   ]

17   If a package contains four boxes of staples and each consecutive box is 50 per cent heavier than the previous one, how heavy is the heaviest box if the total weight of the package is 1 kg? Round your answer up to the nearest gram.

A. 500 g   B. 300 g   C. 450 g

D. 685 g   E. 416 g   F. 725 g

Answer

18   Sales staff A and B are selling the same product. A sold £1,000 worth of product and received 3.5 per cent commission, while B received only 3 per cent. How many more sales should B realize to achieve the same amount of commission as A?

A. £50.67   B. £96.76

C. £116.67   D. £186.76

Answer

19   A videoconference is to take place between Dubai, London and New York. If Dubai is four hours behind London and New York is six hours ahead of London, and if the conference is to start at 2.30 pm on 11 January New York time, what time will it start in Dubai?

A. 00.30 am 10 Jan   B. 02.30 am 10 Jan   C. 00.30 am 11 Jan

D. 02.30 am 11 Jan   E. 04.30 am 11 Jan   F. 02.30 am 12 Jan

Answer

20   Twenty per cent of office workers travel to work by car, 70 per cent by train and 10 per cent by bus. Express these values as a ratio.

A. 2:3.5:1   B. 1:1.6:2   C. 2:2.5:1

D. 2:2.5:1.5   E. 1.5:2.5:1   F. 1:3.5:0.5

Answer

21   Express 3/20 as a percentage.

A. 10%   B. 20%   C. 13.5%

D. 15%   E. 22.5%   F. 35%

Answer

22   One metre of optical fibre cable is priced at £7.99. Calculate the price of one foot of cable, if 1 ft = 0.305 m.

A. £4.50   B. £7.68   C. £2.99

D. £3.99   E. £2.25   F. £2.44

Answer [   ]

23 The maximum weight allowed in the office elevator is 225 kg. What is the maximum weight allowed expressed in lbs, if 1 lb = 0.45 kg?

A. 499.50 lb   B. 500.00 lb   C. 101.25 lb

D. 370.00 lb   E. 350.00 lb   F. 325.00 lb

Answer [   ]

24 If a vehicle travels at 35 mph, how many kilometres would it travel in 30 minutes if 1 km = 0.621 miles?

A. 33 km   B. 56 km   C. 28 km

D. 66 km   E. 18 km   F. 17.5 km

Answer [   ]

25 Kim usually flies from Heathrow, and her taxi fare to the airport is on average £12 for a 25-minute drive. This time, however, Kim is flying from Luton and the taxi drive will take 45 min. Assuming taxi fares are proportionate to the time taken, how much should Kim expect to pay for her drive to Luton airport?

A. £15.60   B. £16.20   C. £21.60

D. £20.60   E. £12.60   F. £6.20

Answer [   ]

26 The price of laminated flooring is £6.25 per sq ft. How much would it cost to buy enough flooring to cover 5 sq m if 1 ft = 0.305 m? Calculate the answer to the nearest pound.

A. £314   B. £150   C. £218

D. £298   E. £336   F. £170

Answer [   ]

27 Frank takes pride in achieving an average of 35 mph during his journey to work of 25 miles. However, in the evening his same journey home takes twice as long. What is Frank's daily average speed?

A. 15.25 mph   B. 25.25 mph   C. 18.25 mph

D. 26.25 mph   E. 30.25 mph   F. 20.25 mph

Answer [   ]

28   In January a project team spent 50 per cent of its total budget plus £1,000. In February 50 per cent of the remainder was spent plus a further £1,000. If at the start of March the project team still had £5,000 of the budgeted amount at its disposal, how much was the total budget assigned?

A. £25,000   B. £26,000   C. £16,000

D. £17,500   E. £24,000   F. £15,000

Answer

29   A shelf in a storage room is 1.83 m wide. How many files can be stored if the width of a single file is 1 inch? (1 inch = 0.083 ft; 1 ft = 0.305 m.)

A. 6   B. 12   C. 60

D. 84   E. 70   F. 72

Answer

30   Marie leaves her house at 7.30 am and arrives at the office at 9 am. If the distance between Marie's house and the office is 56 miles and if she takes a 20-minute break halfway, what is the average speed at which Marie should drive to arrive on time?

A. 45 mph   B. 48 mph   C. 58 mph

D. 37.8 mph   E. 43 mph   F. 27.5 mph

Answer

End of test.

Practice test 2 Data interpretation

This test consists of 24 questions. Allow yourself 20 minutes to complete it.

The tests are made up of a number of tables or graphs of numerical information that are followed by a series of questions relating to each of the tables or graphs. There is a list of suggested answers to each question and it is your task to identify the correct answer. Indicate your answer by writing the letter of the correct answer, A, B, C, D, E or F, in the answer box.

This style of test is becoming extremely common and will test both your ability to interpret information presented graphically and a wide range of numerical competencies. Expect to be tested in, for example, the operation of percentages, ratios, fractions and averages, and the conversion of units of currency or measurements.

Use a calculator if you need to, but try to use it only sparingly. Use scrap paper to do rough workings. Remember to practice educated guessing.

Stick strictly to the recommended time and try hard to get the best possible score.

Do not start until you are ready to begin.

Data interpretation

TABLE 3.1 Market research findings on the preferred colour of pre-paid vouchers

Total no. of interviewees	Age group	Positive responses by preferred colour			
		Green	Blue	Pink	Red
200	15–25	58	45	33	64
200	26–35	68	53	40	39
300	36–45	42	93	70	95
160	46–55	48	56	16	40
90	56–65	25	18	30	17
50	66–75	11	15	10	14

1   Which age group most favoured the green pre-paid vouchers?

A. 15–25   B. 26–35   C. 36–45

D. 46–55   E. 56–65   F. 66–75

Answer

2   How many interviewees most favoured the red vouchers?

A. 113   B. 325   C. 244

D. 269   E. 332   F. 543

Answer

3   What percentage of those aged 15–25 favoured the pink vouchers?

A. 12%   B. 17.5%   C. 22%

D. 16.5%   E. 66.66%   F 33.33%

Answer

4   Which age group was the least favourable to green vouchers in percentage terms?

A. 15–25   B. 26–35   C. 36–45

D. 46–55   E. 56–65   F. 66–75

Answer

Table 3.2 shows the current currency exchange rate into pounds sterling. The commission charged per transaction is 4.5 per cent.

TABLE 3.2 Currency exchange rate into pounds sterling

Country	Currency	Selling price	Buying price	Remarks
Australia	dollar	2.79	2.99	–
Turkey	lira	–	24.49	–
South Africa	rand	3.18	3.38	–
Israel	shekel	–	591.86	500 and above
New Zealand	dollar	5.76	6.18	10 and above
eurozone	euro	1.55	1.66	–

5   Claire went to South Africa and returned with 280 rands. How much will she get, before commission, if she sells them at the current rate?

A. £82.67   B. £75.55   C. £79.11

D. £82.84   E. £88.05   F. £84.08

Answer

6   A company is sending its executives on a business trip to Australia, and the total cash allowance is £1,750. How many Australian dollars can be purchased after paying the commission?

A. 580.78   B. 4,997.03   C. 5,019.88

D. 5,102.21   E. 5,467.96   F. 599.01

Answer

7   The trip to Australia (see Question 6) was cancelled at the last minute, so the company decided to change the unneeded Australian dollars back into pounds. How much in £ sterling did it receive, after paying commission?

A. £1,750.00   B. £1,791.05   C. £13,314.00

D. £1,596.04   E. £1,710.45   F. £4,997.03

Answer

8   Take the average of the selling price and buying price for the euro and use it to calculate 0.5 euros expressed in pounds.

A. £0.31   B. £0.62   C. £0.27

D. £0.95   E. £0.25   F. £0.81

Answer

TABLE 3.3 Bank account holder records

Account holder	Initial balance (£)	Money deposited (£)	Money withdrawn (£)
S Davies	23.45	0	20.00
H Gomez	227.50	50.00	270.00
J K Josef	386.16	12.50	0
O McCormack	−250.00	360.00	25.00
F Wild	−76.50	50.00	0
D Zair	36.00	6.00	40.00

9   What percentage of account holders are overdrawn?

A. 15%   B. 33.33%   C. 19%

D. 16.66%   E. 24.5%   F. 17.5%

Answer

10   If F Wild deposits £2 every fortnight, makes no more withdrawals and is charged no interest or fees, how many weeks will it take before his overdraft is paid off in full?

A. 13.2   B. 53   C. 6.6

D. 12.3   E. 25.6   F. 26.5

Answer

11   If S Davies's salary of £800 is deposited on 4 February and her rent of £95 is debited on the same day, what will her balance be on 5 February?

A. £750.00   B. £709.45   C. £708.45

D. £705.00   E. £728.50   F. £748.00

Answer

12   What is O McCormack's final balance?

A. £85.00   B. £155.00   C. £135.00

D. £90.00   E. £45.00   F. £68.00

Answer

TABLE 3.4 Postage rates

UK	Weight up to:	60g	100g	150g	200g	300g	400g	500g	Each extra 250g
	First class (£)	0.27	0.41	0.57	0.72	0.96	1.30	1.66	0.85
	Second class (£)	0.19	0.33	0.44	0.54	0.76	1.05	–	–
Worldwide	Weight up to:	10g	20g	40g	60g	80g	100g	Each extra 50g	
	Europe	x	0.37	0.52	0.68	0.84	0.99	0.59	
	W Zone 1	0.47	0.68	1.05	1.42	1.79	2.16	1.25	
	W Zone 2	0.47	0.68	1.12	1.56	2.00	2.44	1.40	

13 A first-class package to Aberdeen weighs 550 g and a letter to France weights 12 g. According to Table 3.4, how much is the total postage?

A. £2.03   B. £2.55   C. £2.88

D. £2.50   E. £3.00   F. £3.88

Answer [   ]

14 A first-class package to Dover weighs 0.96 kg. How much is the total postage?

A. £3.36   B. £2.51   C. £3.15

D. £2.15   E. £2.36   F. £3.51

Answer [   ]

15 A packet to Europe is three-and-a-half times lighter than a 350 g packet to the UK, posted first class. How much would it cost to post both packets?

A. £1.95   B. £4.30   C. £2.12

D. £3.50   E. £3.29   F. £2.29

Answer [   ]

16 A first letter to W Zone 1 weighs 40 g, and a second letter to the same destination weighs 65 g. What would the difference in price be if the letters were sent together as a single letter or separately?

A. £1.18   B. £1.23   C. £0.26

D. £0.47   E. £0.57   F. £0.95

Answer [   ]

TABLE 3.5 Birth and mortality rates, 2001

Country	Population in millions	Births per thousand	Deaths per thousand
Germany	83	9.15	9.2
France	60	12	9
Italy	58	9.05	10.05
Spain	40	9.25	9.15
United Kingdom	60	11.54	10.35
Holland	16	8.69	7.85

17 What was the total number of deaths in Germany during the year?

A. 9,200   B. 763,600   C. 92,000

D. 76,300   E. 7,630   F. 184,000

Answer _____

18 What was the total increase in population in France?

A. 720,000   B. 180,000   C. 300,000

D. 18,000   E. 72,000   F. 640,000

Answer _____

19 If the population growth per year remained the same, what would the total French population have been at the end of 2002?

A. 60,360,000   B. 60,000,360   C. 60,360,540

D. 60,366,000   E. 63,600,000   F. 63,654,000

Answer _____

20 Which countries are experiencing a decrease in population?

A. France and   B. United Kingdom   C. Spain and
   United Kingdom   and Germany   Italy

D. Holland and   E. Italy and   F. Germany and
   Spain   Germany   France

Answer _____

TABLE 3.6 Areas of land, water and arable land, 2006

Country	Total area (sq km)	Land	Water	Arable land, permanent pastures and woodland (%)
Germany	357,021	349,223	7,798	33
France	547,030	545,630	1,400	33
Italy	301,230	294,020	7,210	31
Spain	504,782	499,542	5,240	30
England	244,820	241,590	3,230	25
Holland	41,526	33,883	7,643	25

21   How many sq km of land are there in France if you exclude the arable land, permanent pasture and woodlands?

A. 113,810 sq km   B. 192,700 sq km   C. 366,510 sq km

D. 180,058 sq km   E. 118,410 sq km   F. 365,572 sq km

Answer [   ]

22   What is the total area of Holland expressed in sq miles, if 1 mile = 1.6 km? Round your answer to the nearest sq mile.

A. 19,125 sq ml   B. 27,750 sq ml   C. 16,195 sq ml

D. 27,075 sq ml   E. 27,065 sq ml   F. 18,195 sq ml

Answer [   ]

23   What percentage of Holland's total territory is covered by water?

A. 17%   B. 0.17%   C. 1.3%

D. 12.3%   E. 9.5%   F. 18.4%

Answer [   ]

24   What area of total Spanish territory is covered by arable land, permanent pastures and woodland?

A. 253,445.00 sq km   B. 353,347.50 sq km   C. 355,723.50 sq km

D. 188,670.00 sq km   E. 199,887.00 sq km   F. 151,434.50 sq km

Answer [   ]

End of test.

Practice test 3 Correct sentences

This test comprises 20 questions. Allow yourself eight minutes to complete it.

Each question comprises a number of versions of the same sentence, only one of which is correct in terms of English usage. Your task is to identify the correct sentence. Indicate your answer by writing the letter of the correct answer, A, B, C or D, in the answer box.

Stick strictly to the recommended time limit. Try to manage your time so that you finish all the questions and work as fast as you can until you have answered all the questions or run out of time.

Do not start until you are ready to begin.

Correct sentences

1   A. If she's only listened to me, this would never have happened.

 B. If she had only listened to me, this would never have happened.

 C. If she will only listen to me, this will never have happened.

 D. None of these.

Answer

2   A. There's just three thing's you need to know about Jack.

 B. There's just three things you need to know about Jack.

 C. There are just three things you need to know about Jack.

 D. None of these.

Answer

3   A. If I was you I've seen a doctor.

 B. If I were you I'd see a doctor.

 C. If I was you I'll see a doctor.

 D. None of these.

Answer

4   A. It looks like everyone has gone to the cinema.

 B. It looked like everyone has gone to the cinema.

 C. It looks like everyone had gone to the cinema.

 D. None of these.

Answer

5   A. Either Jane or her sister are bringing the dessert.

 B. Either Jane or her sister is bringing the dessert.

 C. Either Jane or her sister were bringing the dessert.

 D. None of these.

Answer

6   A. If I hadn't had my seatbelt on I'll be dead.

 B. If I didn't have my seatbelt on I'll have been dead.

 C. If I hadn't had my seatbelt on I would be dead.

 D. None of these.

Answer

7   A. From Thursday you cannot have either the blue nor the black pens.

B. From Thursday you cannot have either the blue or the black pens.

C. From Thursday you cannot have neither the blue nor the black pens.

D. None of these.

Answer [   ]

8   A. I have been informed that neither Mandy nor Helen will be able to be there on Saturday.

B. I have been informed that neither Mandy or Helen will be able to be there on Saturday.

C. I have been informed that not either Mandy or Helen will be able to be there on Saturday.

D. None of these.

Answer [   ]

9   A. Owning a dog is very different to owning a cat.

B. Owning a dog is very different from owning a cat.

C. Owning a dog is very different over owning a cat.

D. None of these.

Answer [   ]

10   A. Compared with analogue TV, digital TV provided the consumer with a greater choice of programmes to watch.

B. Compared to analogue TV, digital TV providing the consumer with a greater choice of programmes to watch.

C. Compared to analogue TV, digital TV provided the consumer with a greater choice of programmes to watch.

D. None of these.

Answer [   ]

11   A. If you was to go fishing at night you will find that you caught more fish than during the day.

B. If you was to go fishing at night you might find that you catch more fish than during the day.

C. If you were to go fishing at night you might find that you caught more fish than during the day.

D. None of these.

Answer [   ]

12 A. Although the house and barn are on the same property, they will be sold separately.

B. Although the house and barn were on the same property, they will be sold separately.

C. Although the house and barn was on the same property, they were to be sold separately.

D. None of these.

Answer [   ]

13 A. The school have insisted that no child leaves the playground until their parent arrive.

B. The school has insisted that no children leaves the playground until their parent arrives.

C. The school have insisted that no child leaves the playground until their parent arrived.

D. None of these.

Answer [   ]

14 A. The managing director wanted you and I to attend the meeting.

B. The managing director wanted you and me to attend the meeting.

C. The managing director wanted me and you to attend the meeting.

D. None of these.

Answer [   ]

15 A. Each night before I go to bed I made myself a cup of cocoa.

B. Each night before I go to bed I make myself a cup of cocoa.

C. Each night before I go to bed I makes myself a cup of cocoa.

D. None of these.

Answer [   ]

16 A. Carol thought it an honour to receive an MBE.

B. Carol thought it a honour to receive an MBE.

C. Carol thought it an honour to receive a MBE.

D. None of these.

Answer [   ]

17   A. It looks like it's going to rain.

B. It looks like it's about to rain.

C. It looks as if it is going to rain.

D. None of these.

Answer

18   A. Every one of the new computers in the main office have been virus checked.

B. Every one of the new computers in the main office has been virus checked.

C. Every one of the new computers in the main office been virus checked.

D. None of these.

Answer

19   A. It is equally important to check your credit card statement as it is your bank statement.

B. It is equally as important to cheque your credit card statement as it is your bank statement.

C. It is equally as important to check your credit card statement as it is your bank statement.

D. None of these.

Answer

20   A. Mike seems to always do it that way.

B. Mike seems to do it that way always.

C. Mike always seems to do it that way.

D. None of these.

Answer

End of test.

Practice test 4 Following procedures

There are 17 questions to be completed in 12 minutes.

In this test you are provided with some information, such as an organizational chart or description of a hypothetical situation, and some rules that apply to how you should proceed. Below each set of information and rules is a series of questions that you must answer by referring to the information and rules. Each question includes a list of suggested answers. Note that for some questions more than one suggested answer may be correct. Indicate your answer by writing the letter(s) of the correct answer(s) in the answer box.

Keep to the recommended time limit.

Do not start until you are ready to begin.

Following procedures

Situation 1

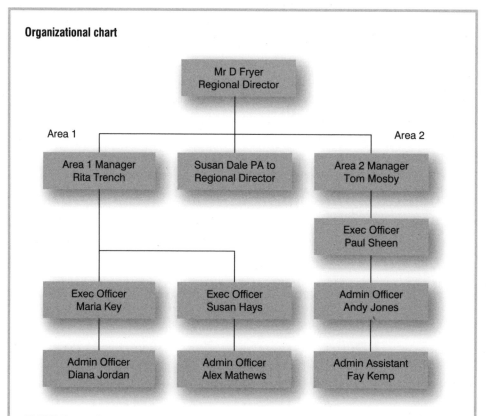

Organizational chart

Mr D Fryer
Regional Director

Area 1

Area 2

Area 1 Manager
Rita Trench

Susan Dale PA to
Regional Director

Area 2 Manager
Tom Mosby

Exec Officer
Paul Sheen

Exec Officer
Maria Key

Exec Officer
Susan Hays

Admin Officer
Andy Jones

Admin Officer
Diana Jordan

Admin Officer
Alex Mathews

Admin Assistant
Fay Kemp

FIGURE 3.1 Organizational chart

List of approved suppliers
Wittlys plc
Echomax UK
Dublin Bay Supplies
Docklands Electrical
Global Solutions Inc

Rules governing purchases in a procurement department
Staff may approve any purchase subject to the following limitations:
- All purchases over £100,000 must be approved by the appropriate area manager and by Mr D Fryer.
- All purchases from a supplier not on the approved-supplier list can only be approved by the area manager.
- Area managers may approve expenditure in their area and from approved suppliers up to a value of £100,000, or for other areas from approved suppliers up to a value of £70,000.

- Within their area, and only with approved suppliers, executive officers may approve purchases to a maximum of £5,000, and administrative officers may approve purchases to a maximum of £1,000.
- Administrative assistants may not approve purchases over £199.
- Susan Dale may approve expenditure to a value of £70,000.

1   Name the member(s) of staff who can approve a purchase for £200 from Island Consultants.

A. Susan Dale   B. Susan Hays   C. Andy Jones

D. Fay Kemp   E. Mr D Fryer   F. Rita French

Answer [_____]

2   Which officer or manager (not director) can approve a purchase of £80,000 for Area 2 from Global Solutions Inc?

A. Rita French   B. Tom Mosby   C. Maria Key

D. Susan Hays   E. Paul Sheen   F. Diana Jordan

G. Alex Matthews   H. Andy Jones

Answer [_____]

3   Which administrative officer(s) can approve a purchase from Wittlys plc for Area 1 to the value of £1,000?

A. Diana Jordan   B. Alex Matthews   C. Andy Jones   D. none

Answer [_____]

4   Which of the following may not approve a purchase of £70,000 for Area 1 from Echomax UK?

A. regional director   B. Susan Dale   C. Rita French

D. Tom Mosby   E. Maria Key

Answer [_____]

5   How many of the following staff are required to approve a purchase of over £100,000 from Dockland Electrical for Area 2?

Mr D Fryer, Susan Dale, Rita French, Tom Mosby, Maria Key, Susan Hays, Paul Sheen

A. 1   B. 2   C. 3   D. 4   E. 5   F. 6   G. 7

Answer [_____]

Situation 2

Robin commissioned an employment agency to fill a position in his company. The agency's fees are based on a percentage of the first year's remuneration. The agency's terms allow for them to add tax to the total due at 15 per cent.

The terms of business of the agency stated that:

- Fixed-term contracts are charged at an apportioned pro-rata basis of permanent fees.
- If the introduced employee leaves within eight weeks of starting employment, a 100 per cent rebate applies; if the employee leaves after eight weeks and before 12 weeks, a 50 per cent rebate applies; if the employee leaves after 12 weeks but before 20 weeks, a 25 per cent rebate is given.
- If the remuneration includes the provision of a car, the sum of £2,000 shall be added to the first year's remuneration for purposes of calculating the introduction fee (irrespective of whether the contract is permanent or fixed term).
- For annual remuneration up to £15,999, the introduction fee is 16 per cent; between £16,000 and £19,999, it is 20 per cent; and over £20,000 it is 25 per cent.

6   What percentage would be used to calculate the introduction fee if the position to be filled was permanent, and paid £20,000 a year with no other benefits?

A. 16%   B. 20%   C. 25%   D. insufficient information to tell

Answer [   ]

7   If after 10 weeks of employment the introduced employee left the company's employment, what kind of rebate should Robin expect on the bill?

A. 100%   B. 50%   C. 25%   D. none

Answer [   ]

8   What fee should Robin expect if the employee was to start on a fixed-term contract of employment for a term of six months on a salary of £16,000 per annum plus the benefit of a car?

A. insufficient information to answer

B. 20% of £16,000 ÷ 2 (apportioned pro-rata reduction for six-month fixed term)

C. 25% of 18,000 ÷ 2 (apportioned pro-rata reduction for six-month fixed term)

D. 20% of 18,000 ÷ 2 (apportioned pro-rata reduction for six-month fixed term)

E. 25% of £9,000 plus 15% tax

F. 20% of £10,000 plus 15% tax

Answer ⬚

Situation 3

Mrs Smith is the manager of the accounts-due department in a busy builders' merchants. She has an assistant, Tina, and between them they are responsible for issuing 10,000 invoices a year and collecting payments against them. Mrs Smith's line manager is Mr Jones, the company accountant, with whom she meets weekly. At this meeting they review all accounts on which an invoice is overdue and all disputed invoices, and decide whether or not to refer an account to the company's firm of solicitors for advice as to whether there is a case for issuing legal proceedings. (Mrs Smith is responsible for carrying out all the decisions made at this meeting except the issuing of legal proceedings, which is done by a firm of solicitors.)

It is the responsibility of sales staff to ensure that all customers agree to the company's terms of business before the company will accept an order. Sales staff may not accept further orders from customers whose accounts have any overdue invoices against them.

Mrs Smith and her assistant operate according to the following procedures:
- The company's terms of business state that payment must be received within 15 working days of the receipt of goods and that notice of faulty or incomplete goods must be given within 5 working days.
- Invoices are issued on the same day as the goods are dispatched; the first reminder is sent out after 5 working days and the final reminder on the 15th working day, notifying the customer that the invoice is overdue and that payment must be made immediately.

---

9 What action(s) should Mrs Smith take if a new customer has failed to pay an invoice within 15 working days of receipt of the goods?

A. Refer the customer to the appointed firm of solicitors.

B. Confirm with sales staff that the customer did indeed agree to the terms of business before the order was accepted.

C. Issue a reminder.

D. Refuse any further orders from that customer.

E. Resolve to review the account with Mr Jones at their next meeting.

Answer [   ]

10   Whose responsibility is it to collect payments against the 10,000 invoices issued each year?

A. Mr Jones   B. Mrs Smith   C. The sales staff   D. Tina

E. It is not possible to say

Answer [   ]

11   Mr Jones and Mrs Smith decide whether or not to:

A. Issue legal proceedings against disputed invoices.

B. Issue legal proceedings against overdue invoices.

C. Issue legal proceedings against both disputed and overdue invoices.

D. None of these.

Answer [   ]

Situation 4

An applicant to an industrial tribunal complained that she had been the victim of sexual discrimination on the grounds that she had received a lower percentage salary increase than some of her male colleagues. In deciding the case, the tribunal referred to the following rules. Use them to answer the questions that follow.

Rules

1   It is for the applicant to make out his or her case on the balance of probabilities.

2   It is unusual to find direct evidence of sexual discrimination, and few employers will be prepared to admit such discrimination.

3   The outcome of a case depends on what inferences it is proper to draw from the primary facts found by the tribunal.

4   A finding of discrimination and a finding of a difference in gender will often point to the possibility of sexual discrimination. In such circumstances the tribunal will look to the employer for an explanation.

5   At the conclusion of all the evidence the tribunal should reach a conclusion, bearing in mind the difficulties that face a person who complains of unlawful discrimination and the fact that it is for the complainant to prove his or her case.

12   Which of the following pieces of information would least support the applicant's case?

A. The applicant was unable to present evidence of direct discrimination on the ground of gender.

B. The employer denied discrimination on the ground of gender.

C. The tribunal concluded that the applicant was unable to prove her case on the balance of probability.

D. The employer admitted indirectly discriminating on the basis of gender.

Answer [   ]

13   What would you expect the tribunal to do if the applicant demonstrated on the balance of probability that she had been treated differently?

A. Ask the employer to explain the unequal treatment.

B. Conclude that the employer had discriminated unfairly.

C. Award an unlimited sum in compensation.

D. Conclude that direct discrimination on the grounds of gender had taken place.

E. None of these.

Answer [   ]

14   Which piece of information would best explain the tribunal's conclusion that the applicant's claim had failed?

A. Evidence presented showed that she had received a 3 per cent increase, in line with most other employees.

B. The employer provided explanations to demonstrate that the exceptions were all for good reason.

C. Mr Smith had had a higher percentage increase to bring him up to the same salary as the applicant, and had been paid too little before that pay rise.

D. Mr Gamble had received no pay rise at all because his recent review had found him to be ineffective in his post.

Answer [   ]

Situation 5

A stakeholder pension is a tax-efficient way of saving specifically for retirement. Savers are provided with their own plan and are sent regular statements showing the value of their fund. Use the stated rules to answer the questions that follow.

Rules

1 All contributions to a stakeholder's pension plan qualify for tax relief at the highest rate paid by the saver, and growth is free of UK income tax and capital gains tax.

2 Fund values are calculated daily.

3 Management charges are due and calculated each day on the basis of the value of the fund on that day. The fee is based on 1/365th of the appropriate rate of the annual management fee.

4 Providers charge according to a tiered series of charges, with qualifying levels dependent on the saver's fund value:

  – For funds valued at up to £15,000 the fee is 1.25 per cent.

  – For funds valued between £15,000 and £24,999 the fee is 1 per cent.

  – For funds valued between £25,000 and £50,000 the fee is 0.8 per cent.

  – For funds valued at over £50,000 the fee is 0.6 per cent.

15 What level of management charge will a stakeholder pension provider make against a saver with a fund valued at £50,000?

A. 1.25%   B. 1%   C. 0.8%   D. 0.6%

Answer

16 Stakeholder pension providers are not allowed to charge more than a maximum annual management fee of 1.25 per cent of the fund value.

A. True   B. False   C. Cannot tell

Answer

17 A saver complains that he has been overcharged as a management fee of 1/365th of 1 per cent per day was applied to his fund with a value of £14,000; is he right in his assertion?

A. Yes, he has been overcharged.

B. No, he has not been overcharged.

C. The calculation is correct.

D. It is not possible to tell.

Answer

End of test.

Practice test 5 Speed and accuracy

This test has 50 questions to be attempted in six minutes.

Each question comprises four pairs of numbers and letters arranged in two columns. It is your task to identify how many pairs of numbers and letters are identical in both columns. You are offered five possible answers: one pair, two pairs, three pairs, four pairs or none. Indicate your answer by writing the letter of the correct answer, A, B, C, D or E, in the answer box.

This is obviously a test of working fast and accurately.

With practice you can greatly improve your speed in this type of test.

Keep strictly to the suggested time limit and stop when the time is up.

Do not start until you are ready to begin.

Speed and accuracy

1   YRCK2971   YRCK2971
9020PXZ3   9020PXZ3
ALGY8431   ALGV8431
467111PQK   46711PQK

A. 1 pair   B. 2 pairs   C. 3 pairs   D. 4 pairs   E. none

Answer [ ]

2   0000412P   0000412P
12123DF   12113DF
XXYG772   XXYG772
LLXII110   LLXII110

A. 1 pair   B. 2 pairs   C. 3 pairs   D. 4 pairs   E. none

Answer [ ]

3   UIUA297   UIUA297
0021ZPW   0021ZPW
BJUH211   BJUH121
99741ILS   99741ILS

A. 1 pair   B. 2 pairs   C. 3 pairs   D. 4 pairs   E. none

Answer [ ]

4   LSAT44211   LSAT42211
1911CCRE   1191CCRE
AAA00031   AAAA0031
VTRE7421   VTER7421

A. 1 pair   B. 2 pairs   C. 3 pairs   D. 4 pairs   E. none

Answer [ ]

5   LLL6770   LLL6110
AKAKI21   AKAKL12
00003321   00003221
XXREWQ   XXREWQ

A. 1 pair   B. 2 pairs   C. 3 pairs   D. 4 pairs   E. none

Answer [ ]

6   999321SS   999321SS
       01023WQK   01023WQK
       876345CF   876345CF
       1111874RE   1111874RE

A. 1 pair   B. 2 pairs   C. 3 pairs   D. 4 pairs   E. none

Answer [   ]

7   975985AS   975985AS
       AS975985   AS975985
       97AS5958   97AS5958
       AS599785   AS975985

A. 1 pair   B. 2 pairs   C. 3 pairs   D. 4 pairs   E. none

Answer [   ]

8   50515052Q   50515052Q
       456789CCF   457689CCF
       XOIU1113   XOUI1113
       AAAKI334   AAKII334

A. 1 pair   B. 2 pairs   C. 3 pairs   D. 4 pairs   E. none

Answer [   ]

9   QQWE4456   QQWU4456
       754BBRT1   754BBTR1
       8UWQ321   8UQW321
       BEWQ908   BEWO908

A. 1 pair   B. 2 pairs   C. 3 pairs   D. 4 pairs   E. none

Answer [   ]

10   VVVTT332   VVVT3332
       CCCV8871   CCCW8871
       33541FFDE   333451FFDE
       4498XXEW   4988XXEW

A. 1 pair   B. 2 pairs   C. 3 pairs   D. 4 pairs   E. none

Answer [   ]

11   11221ZZW   11221ZZW
       ZZWW1122   ZZWW1122
       11ZZWW22   11ZWWW22
       222ZZWW1   222ZZWW1

A. 1 pair   B. 2 pairs   C. 3 pairs   D. 4 pairs   E. none

Answer [   ]

12 XDMK2220   XDMK2200
   NNNJU454   NNNJU545
   ZWPL0081   ZWPL0811
   NNJU2121   NNJU1212
   A. 1 pair   B. 2 pairs   C. 3 pairs   D. 4 pairs   E. none

   Answer

13 LLKII2245   LLKII2445
   2445KIILL   2245KIILL
   LKL11245   LKL12145
   12145LKL   12145LKL
   A. 1 pair   B. 2 pairs   C. 3 pairs   D. 4 pairs   E. none

   Answer

14 OOOO332   OOO3332
   33220000Q   3322000Q
   O332Q000   O332Q000
   OOOQ233   OOOQ233
   A. 1 pair   B. 2 pairs   C. 3 pairs   D. 4 pairs   E. none

   Answer

15 LOLL2231   LOL22231
   77208XKX   77280XKX
   AW34KI81   AW34KI81
   CC873KIQ   CC837KIQ
   A. 1 pair   B. 2 pairs   C. 3 pairs   D. 4 pairs   E. none

   Answer

16 HUHI5467   HUHI5467
   QPAL2881   QPAL2881
   2313XRV1   2313XRV1
   99921VTR   99921VTR
   A. 1 pair   B. 2 pairs   C. 3 pairs   D. 4 pairs   E. none

   Answer

17 000112XD   001112XD
   XD110002   XD11002
   CRRC343   CRRC343
   2323VVG   2323VVG
   A. 1 pair   B. 2 pairs   C. 3 pairs   D. 4 pairs   E. none

   Answer

18   874301VWV   873401VWV
     ZZZ220011   ZZ2220011
     2220011XX   222011XX
     LPPI09111   LPPI09111

A. 1 pair   B. 2 pairs   C. 3 pairs   D. 4 pairs   E. none

Answer

19   00873BBHU   00878BBHU
     BBUH00738   BPUH00738
     BPUH78700   BPUH87800
     BBHU78700   BPUH78700

A. 1 pair   B. 2 pairs   C. 3 pairs   D. 4 pairs   E. none

Answer

20   984560XXY   985460XXY
     77442CCG1   77442CCG1
     00101X0X1   00101X0X1
     020274V0V   020274V0V

A. 1 pair   B. 2 pairs   C. 3 pairs   D. 4 pairs   E. none

Answer

21   00000333   0000333
     3333000   33330000
     1110001   11100001
     1000001   10000001

A. 1 pair   B. 2 pairs   C. 3 pairs   D. 4 pairs   E. none

Answer

22   HH2349EW   HH2349EW
     VV8815829   VV8814829
     18357AEM   18857AEM
     AEMM3921   AEM3921

A. 1 pair   B. 2 pairs   C. 3 pairs   D. 4 pairs   E. none

Answer

23   SS32109UI   SS32109UI
     459821XFL   459821XFL
     NUEE90123   NUEE90123
     CUQOS321   CUQOS321

A. 1 pair   B. 2 pairs   C. 3 pairs   D. 4 pairs   E. none

Answer

24   QOOQW187   QOQOW187
         IVVII23910   IVIIV23910
         UCV.29870   UCV.29870
         XHQ/4002   XHQ\4002

A. 1 pair   B. 2 pairs   C. 3 pairs   D. 4 pairs   E. none

Answer

25   10000011   10000011
         33300000   33300000
         66000006   66000006
         99999911   99999911

A. 1 pair   B. 2 pairs   C. 3 pairs   D. 4 pairs   E. none

Answer

26   PO89XV22   PO89XV22
         LPCDDVDM3   LPCDDVDMP3
         999101EMG   99101EMG
         10.901.87   10.0109.87

A. 1 pair   B. 2 pairs   C. 3 pairs   D. 4 pairs   E. none

Answer

27   10.901.87   10.901.87
         10.901.88   10.901.88
         10.901.89   10.901.90
         10.901.90   10.901.91

A. 1 pair   B. 2 pairs   C. 3 pairs   D. 4 pairs   E. none

Answer

28   WA427319A   WA427139A
         QS982309B   QS892309B
         CV459889A   CV459889A
         ZX923405B   XZ923405B

A. 1 pair   B. 2 pairs   C. 3 pairs   D. 4 pairs   E. none

Answer

29   \0910PE33D   0910PE33D
         D880PE106/   D880PE106\
         \091D8833P   \91D8333P
         D01YE107/   D10YE107/

A. 1 pair   B. 2 pairs   C. 3 pairs   D. 4 pairs   E. none

Answer

30   AAAAIIII   AAAAIIII
         IIIIIAAAA   IIIIIAAAA
         AIAIAIAI   AIAIAIA
         AAAIIIAA   AAAIIAA

A. 1 pair   B. 2 pairs   C. 3 pairs   D. 4 pairs   E. none

Answer

31   5LN5COL17   5LN5COL17
         13 15111 04   13 1551 04
         27 1862 07   27 1826 07
         787 2935 72   787 2935 72

A. 1 pair   B. 2 pairs   C. 3 pairs   D. 4 pairs   E. none

Answer

32   KMK16–Q001   KMK16–Q001
         KMK-BBOB1   KMK-BBOB1
         KMMME352   KMMME352
         KMK14–N010PC   KMK14–N010PC

A. 1 pair   B. 2 pairs   C. 3 pairs   D. 4 pairs   E. none

Answer

33   KMPB50024V   KMBP50012V
         LED5MM12V   LED4MM12V
         DJZI24140A   DJZI24140A
         VSDRPCSV   VSDRPCSV

A. 1 pair   B. 2 pairs   C. 3 pairs   D. 4 pairs   E. none

Answer

34   K6.5   EFOZ   K6.5EFOZ
         K27EFOZSS   K27EFOZSS
         DJZL24140A   DJZL24120A
         EPOS24VDC   EPOS240VDC

A. 1 pair   B. 2 pairs   C. 3 pairs   D. 4 pairs   E. none

Answer

35   800000011   80000011
         62222299   62222999
         77771110   77771110
         55555999   55555999

A. 1 pair   B. 2 pairs   C. 3 pairs   D. 4 pairs   E. none

Answer

36 A00RGS3B11   A00RGSB311
Q01SP1B16   Q01PS1B16
24V2X100   24V2X100
100W24VSP33   10W24VSP33

A. 1 pair   B. 2 pairs   C. 3 pairs   D. 4 pairs   E. none

Answer

37 MEAMM30/2   MEAMM32/0
MEAMM32/0   MEAMM30/2
AQUAIR100   AQUAIRR100
SRPV7D12   SRPV7D12

A. 1 pair   B. 2 pairs   C. 3 pairs   D. 4 pairs   E. none

Answer

38 SRCMLPV7D   SRCMLPV7D
SPUS116FC   SPUS116FC
W01SPA00RG   W01SPA00RG
A00RGDB19   A00RGDB19

A. 1 pair   B. 2 pairs   C. 3 pairs   D. 4 pairs   E. none

Answer

39 INV32008   INV320008
INV320008   INV32008
INV3756   INV3576
INV8532   INV8523

A. 1 pair   B. 2 pairs   C. 3 pairs   D. 4 pairs   E. none

Answer

40 77777222   777777222
00000004   00000044
1000004   10000004
5666633   5666333

A. 1 pair   B. 2 pairs   C. 3 pairs   D. 4 pairs   E. none

Answer

41 3981CH10.20   3981CH10.20
3944a22.58   3944a22.58
NR210020mm   NR210020mm
NR207MOKKEN NR207MOKKERK

A. 1 pair   B. 2 pairs   C. 3 pairs   D. 4 pairs   E. none

Answer

42   BY313634X6X6.5   BY313643X6X6.5
BY29521.5X9X9.5   BY29512.5X9X9.5
BY21.5X9X7   BY21.5X9X7
BY38.6X9X4.3   BY38.6X9X4.3

A. 1 pair   B. 2 pairs   C. 3 pairs   D. 4 pairs   E. none

Answer

43   303579×65×7F   303579×65×7F
204360×16×1.8   204360×16×1.8
3057 San Remo   3057 San Remo
3057 Mallorca   3057 Mallorca

A. 1 pair   B. 2 pairs   C. 3 pairs   D. 4 pairs   E. none

Answer

44   SGT031LICTHGEN   SGT031LICTHGEN
SGTO31VERWEND   SGTO31VERWEND
SIE VERWENDEN   SIE VERWENDEN
TO040PORTILEN   TO040PORTILEN

A. 1 pair   B. 2 pairs   C. 3 pairs   D. 4 pairs   E. none

Answer

45   0000000555   000000555
555555000   5555555000
050505050   05050505050
50505050   50505050505

A. 1 pair   B. 2 pairs   C. 3 pairs   D. 4 pairs   E. none

Answer

46   WDKX10PVC   WCKX10PVC
WDKXO9RB   WDKX09PVC
WDKX08PVC   WDKXO9PVC
WDKX07RB   WKDX07RB

A. 1 pair   B. 2 pairs   C. 3 pairs   D. 4 pairs   E. none

Answer

47   68969657   68969 657
68969660   68969657
68969 662   68969662
68969 658   68969 658

A. 1 pair   B. 2 pairs   C. 3 pairs   D. 4 pairs   E. none

Answer

48   205×100×16   205×100×16
           380×85×75   38×850×75
           500×250×150   500×250×150
           240×68×125   240×68×125

           A. 1 pair   B. 2 pairs   C. 3 pairs   D. 4 pairs   E. none

           Answer

49   LH201WHG4   LH201WHG4
           LH160BRUHAN   LH160GRNHAN
           LH92GRNHAN   LH92BRUHAN
           LH140BLUHAN   LH140BLUHAN

           A. 1 pair   B. 2 pairs   C. 3 pairs   D. 4 pairs   E. none

           Answer

50   00000001   0000001
           1111110   11111110
           11100001   11100011
           00001110   00011100

           A. 1 pair   B. 2 pairs   C. 3 pairs   D. 4 pairs   E. none

           Answer

End of test.

CHAPTER 4

Non-Fast Stream managerial grades

Appointment to many (non-Fast Stream) managerial and higher managerial positions in the Civil Service involves a type of assessment not covered in any other part of this title. These assessments are called situational tests, personality questionnaires and attitudinal tests. Such tests and questionnaires can take as much as one-and-a-half hours to complete. They are very different in nature from other sorts of psychometric assessment and provide a report on attributes and characteristics regarding your personal and managerial style. Take this to mean that the Civil Service will use your responses to build a psychometric profile of your attitude and personality. While people may be reluctant to call them tests and they say no answer is right or wrong, the profile they build is used to decide if your application should be accepted or rejected, so take the questions seriously.

Some people mistakenly believe that you cannot improve your performance in this style of tests. You can, because many people rush them and do not give the statements they comprise sufficient consideration.

It is essential in this type of exercise that you answer the questions truthfully but it is equally essential that you keep at the front of your mind the context of the questions. You are applying for a managerial position within the Civil Service and it is in this context that you are answering the questions. With each question ask yourself: 'As an applicant to a managerial position in the Civil Service, how would I respond in that situation?' Take the example: 'I would describe myself as tactful.' You should be able to answer this question positively. You might be able to think up some situation when you would not describe yourself as tactful, perhaps when out with your friends or at home with your family. But this would be the totally wrong response in the context of the question. How you sometimes act with your friends or family is irrelevant to your role as a manager in the Civil Service. In such a position tact is essential and candidates who cannot describe themselves as tactful may not be selected.

Responding truthfully to the questions will sometimes mean that you admit to something that risks counting against you. For example, if you have not undertaken voluntary work and you are asked if you have, be prepared to say that you have not. Generally speaking, a few negative-scoring answers will not usually significantly affect your overall score; and anyway, if you lie and it is discovered at a later stage, your application may be rejected.

Below are 90 practice questions for three styles of question.

Situational awareness tests

Situational awareness tests comprise a passage in which an imaginary workplace situation is described and lists suggested responses to that situation. Your task is to rank the suggested responses as the most appropriate, acceptable or less than acceptable. In the practice examples below there are more suggested responses than categories in which you can rank them. This means that you must rank more than one response the same. Enter your rankings in the answer matrix. Be sure that you only refer to the information provided in the situation and do not bring to your deliberations imaginary responses which for example you might consider better. In other words, use only your own best judgement and the information provided to decide the rankings.

Identify as the most appropriate the response that you consider is the best of those suggested. If you consider two or more of the suggested responses the most appropriate, then do not rank any of the answers as A but instead rank them as B, an acceptable response. It is possible that you do not consider any of the suggested responses the most appropriate or acceptable, in which case do not rank any of the answers as A or B.

Answers and explanations are provided in Chapter 8. To score your answers, award yourself a maximum of four marks per question, one mark for each correct ranking you attribute to each suggested response.

Situation 1

You are entering the building where you work and find a man standing at the door. The door requires a pass to be placed over a pad before it opens and you use your pass to unlock the door. Without thinking, you hold the door open for the person who enters with you and thanks you. He looks smart and businesslike but you do not recognize him. This does not mean that he does not work in the building or should not be inside, as many people work there and you do not know them all. You decide to ask to see his security pass but he refuses and tells you that he works in security and that he does not have to show his pass.

Rate the suggested responses as:

A. The most appropriate response

B. An acceptable response

C. A less than acceptable response

The suggested responses:

1 Ask his name and go to your office and call security to check if it is true that he works there.

2 Politely insist that he shows you his pass.

3 Offer to accompany him to the office of the security team so that they may confirm he works there.

4 Let the matter drop.

Your answer:

1	2	3	4

Situation 2

A colleague complains to you about the body odour of a member of your team. On a few occasions you have noticed the bad odour yourself but decided against saying anything as you are aware of some personal difficulties that the individual faces.

Rate the suggested responses as:

A. The most appropriate response

B. An acceptable response

C. A less than acceptable response

The suggested responses:

1 You would quietly explain to your colleague the nature of the personal problems that the individual faces and ask them to be more understanding.

2 Resolve to raise the matter with the individual at the next team meeting and inform your colleague that you will handle it.

3 Ask your colleague to say no more on the subject and do nothing.

4 Meet privately with the member of your team and ask that they pay more attention to their personal hygiene.

Your answer:

1	2	3	4

Situation 3

You overhear a heated conversation between two members of staff, neither of whom is in your team. You are shocked to hear one of the individuals threaten the other with physical violence. You know both the individuals concerned and can't really believe what you are hearing.
Soon after the threat the individuals become aware of your presence and the conversation abruptly stops.

Rate the suggested responses as:

A. The most appropriate response

B. An acceptable response

C. A less than acceptable response

The suggested responses:

1 You would act as if you had heard nothing and not get involved.

2 You would take the matter up according to the procedure laid down in the staff handbook.

3 You would approach their respective line managers and report the matter to them.

4 You would speak to the two individuals and explain to them what you heard and that you consider it a very serious matter and something they need to sort out between themselves without resort to threats of violence.

Your answer:

1	2	3	4

Situation 4

> You were asked to try and sort out a failing project, the aim of which was to get more 16–18-year-olds to remain in education. The first thing you had to address was the steering group, which comprised representatives of 12 organizations all with competing agendas, priorities and interests. When you attended the first steering-group meeting you realized just how bad things were as each organization had been using it own system to collate results from their activities. This meant that you were presented with 12 different sets of data. The individuals who made up the steering group were highly influential but their morale was low and some declared that they were close to resigning from the group. Your manager had explained to you that if this happened the project would have to close.

Rate the suggested responses as:

A. The most appropriate response

B. An acceptable response

C. A less than acceptable response

The suggested responses:

1 You would address the meeting and offer as compelling a case as possible for the representatives to support you in an attempt to turn things around.

2 You would ask members of the steering group to tell you how the project could be saved.

3 You would immediately set about agreeing with the representatives what is needed to turn the project around and negotiate with both your manager and the representatives to ensure that those resources were made available to the project.

4 You would undertake to collate the 12 sets of data and identify findings that can be inferred across the different sets of data.

Your answer:

1	2	3	4

Situation 5

You criticize a member of your staff for grammatical errors in a report and the individual denies being the author. You realize that you were mistaken but the individual concerned gets extremely angry and starts shouting and using bad language.

Rate the suggested responses as:

A. The most appropriate response

B. An acceptable response

C. A less than acceptable response

The suggested responses:

1 You would interrupt them to instruct them to stop shouting and using bad language, and you would tell them that when they have calmed down you wish to speak to them; then you would then turn away and leave them.

2 You would let them have their say and then apologize and retract your criticism.

3 You would let them finish and calmly tell them not to shout and swear and then you would apologize and retract your criticism.

4 You would interrupt them to stop them and explain that you wished to apologize for your error but that it is entirely unacceptable for them to shout and use bad language, and if they do not stop immediately you will walk away and discuss the matter with them later.

Your answer:

1	2	3	4

Situation 6

The first year of the project had gone well. However, while you encourage your team to take a moment to congratulate themselves you are well aware that it will be considerably harder to repeat the success in year 2. Your caution is based on the fact that the project's year 2 targets are many time higher than those of year 1 and your team will have to raise the game considerably if they are to repeat the success.

Rate the suggested responses as:

A. The most appropriate response

B. An acceptable response

C. A less than acceptable response

The suggested responses:

1 You would circulate an e-mail alerting the team to your concerns and your view that everyone will have to raise the game considerably if the targets for year 2 are to be realized.

2 You would set about undertaking an analysis of year 1 in order to anticipate future trends and inform suitable strategies for the achievement of the year 2 targets.

3 You would call a team meeting to present an analysis of year 1 and what you believe will be the future trends and best strategies in order to achieve the year 2 targets.

4 You would call a team meeting where you review year 1 and present the targets for year 2, and assign to members of the team the task of predicting future trends and the brainstorming of strategies for the achievement of the year 2 targets.

Your answer:

1	2	3	4

Situation 7

Following a reorganization, you have noticed that two of your team who had previously worked well together have started to blame each other for even the slightest problem and now bicker over responsibilities.

Rate the suggested responses as:

A.   The most appropriate response

B.   An acceptable response

C.   A less than acceptable response

The suggested responses:

1 You would call a team meeting and re-communicate the roles assigned to each member of the team at the reorganization.

2 You would call a team meeting and explain that you have noticed that there seems some confusion over roles and responsibilities since the reorganization, and then re-communicate the roles assigned to each member of the team at the reorganization.

3 You would review the assignment of roles to see if there was any unintentional duplication or conflict and meet with the two individuals to discuss what you have noticed and seek their views on whether or not the assignment of roles can be adjusted to avoid doubling up or a clash.

4 You would meet with the two individuals and re-communicate the roles assigned to them at the reorganization.

Your answer:

1	2	3	4

Situation 8

> A visitor to your building reported that their mobile phone and packet of sweets went missing when they left a room that they were using to go to use the toilet facilities. There is a large sign in the room that states that personal belongings should not be left unattended and that the management cannot take any responsibility for any loss or damage to personal items.
>
> The room is covered by a security camera and when you review the footage you observe a member of your staff entering the room and appearing to pick up something from the table. You approach the member of staff and they confess to taking the sweets but deny taking the mobile phone.

Rate the suggested responses as:

A. The most appropriate response

B. An acceptable response

C. A less than acceptable response

The suggested responses:

1 You would call the police and report the theft and tell them that you have CCTV footage that appears to identify the thief, and that a member of staff has admitted to stealing one of the missing items.

2 You would insist that the individual replaces the sweets and apologizes to the visitor; you would also explain to the visitor that there was nothing you could do about the phone and remind them of the content of the sign in the room.

3 You would search the individual's desk and pockets to see if you could locate the phone.

4 You would arrange for a meeting between the visitor and the individual so that they could explain that they only took the sweets and apologize.

Your answer:

1	2	3	4

Situation 9

Nothing was to be gained from trying to lay blame for the fact that 2,000 contracts had been sent out for signature by contractors and an essential clause had been omitted. Fortunately the error had been spotted before the returned contracts had been countersigned and the contracts become legally binding. There was no alternative but to contact each of the organizations by telephone, explain the error and reissue new contracts. It was a large task for your already busy team and time was of the essence because in less than four weeks the project was to go live and before that date all contracts must in place.

Rate the suggested responses as:

A.   The most appropriate response

B.   An acceptable response

C.   A less than acceptable response

The suggested responses:

1 Under the circumstances you would recommend that the project start is delayed.

2 You would call a team meeting to discuss the possibility of contacting all the contractors, reissuing the contracts and ensuring their return within the time available.

3 You would call a meeting of your team and announce that between them they will have to contact all the contractors, reissue the contracts and ensure their return within the time available.

4 You would cancel all your appointments, pick the phone up and immediately start contacting all the contractors and instructing your team to urgently reissue the contracts.

Your answer:

1	2	3	4

Situation 10

Once again the way you organize your team must change. Regrettably this is the third time you have had to reorganize things in as many months and the last time you promised the staff that it would be the last restructuring. You know that the team will resent the need to change once more and you too share the understandable sense of frustration it will give rise to. You have time to call a meeting, after which the reorganization must go ahead.

Rate the suggested responses as:

A.   The most appropriate response

B.   An acceptable response

C.   A less than acceptable response

The suggested responses:

1 You would use the meeting to provide an explanation of the reason for the change.

2 Your would use the meeting to provide a sincere apology for the necessity to change things once again.

3 You would use the meeting to provide the opportunity for staff to vent their frustrations.

4 You would use the meeting to provide clear direction for the reorganization.

Your answer:

1	2	3	4

Situation 11

> You team provides a service seven days a week between the hours of 8 am and 8 pm. This is achieved by working one of two six-hour shifts. One starts at 8 am, the other at 2 pm. One of your staff approaches you to explain that their personal circumstances have changed and they would no longer be able to work at weekends until they have made alternative childcare arrangements.

Rate the suggested responses as:

A. The most appropriate response

B. An acceptable response

C. A less than acceptable response

The suggested responses:

1 You would call a meeting to discuss the person's change of personal circumstances and their request not to work weekends for a period.

2 You would ask them how long it will be before they can return to working weekends and if it is a reasonable length of time you would agree to their request.

3 You would try to organize things differently so that their change of circumstances could be accommodated.

4 You would explain that you must treat everyone equally and that therefore like everyone else they will have to continue to work weekends.

Your answer:

1	2	3	4

Situation 12

You are leading a project to find a new use for redundant Ministry of Defence land. One idea is to construct a wind farm. Planning permission has been sought for the erection of 200 wind turbines and if the project goes ahead it would provide 5 per cent of the power needs of the nearby town of Canning. Local opinion is strongly divided. Some recognize the value of a carbon-free source of power and welcome the few jobs that the project would create. The majority hotly oppose the project because they find the wind turbines unsightly and a danger to the local wild bird population.

Another proposal that you are considering is to site on the land a young offenders' institute for 500 youths convicted of serious antisocial behaviour. The institute would work to rehabilitate the young people. This work would include unsupervised trips into Canning. The proposal for the institute is still confidential and not in the public domain.

You and a representative of the wind farm project attend a public meeting that is heavily attended by opponents to the wind farm's planning application. Much to your surprise and annoyance, in reply to a question the representative of the wind farm project suggests that if residents succeed in preventing the wind farm then they will instead face the prospect of 500 young offenders invading their town and that in his opinion the wind farm is the lesser of two evils.

Rate the suggested responses as:

A.   The most appropriate response

B.   An acceptable response

C.   A less than acceptable response

The suggested responses:

1 You would tell those present that you did not share the view just expressed by the other speaker and that you could only comment on the proposal to use the land for a wind farm.

2 You would say that the rejection of one proposal would not guarantee the success of another but that you could not comment on other proposals because at this stage they were confidential.

3 You would say nothing and after the meeting would privately tell the wind farm representative that he should not have said what he did.

4 You would deny any knowledge of a proposal for a young offender's institute.

Your answer:

1	2	3	4

Situation 13

You manage a national project the objective of which is to encourage under-represented groups to apply to become teachers. Interested individuals must first train at one of a number of teacher training colleges and the colleges have a closing date for applicants in June each year. The project involves a series of national advertisements on billboards, promoting the benefits of a career in teaching. An urgent problem has arisen. The advertising agency responsible for booking the space on the billboards has notified you that the adverts will not appear as agreed during the spring and early summer but instead will appear in the summer and autumn. This means that anyone who responds to the advertisement will have missed the closing date for teacher training and will have to wait a full year before they can start training for a career in teaching. You must find a solution because if you do not, the consequences for your project will be serious.

Rate the suggested responses as:

A.   The most appropriate response

B.   An acceptable response

C.   A less than acceptable response

The suggested responses:

1 Your preference would be to involve all staff in cooperatively developing a practical solution.

2 You would prefer to work on a solution with a number of individuals whom you trust and then present that solution to the whole team.

3 Your preferred approach would be to develop a practical solution with other managers and then present it to the team as a whole.

4 You would prefer to develop a solution yourself and present it to the team for their comments.

Your answer:

1	2	3	4

Situation 14

A member of your team complained of feeling stressed and apprehensive. You arranged to speak to him in private and he explained that he feels most apprehension whenever anything goes wrong at work and that he then feels helpless and unsure how he might help put things right.

Rate the suggested responses as:

A. The most appropriate response

B. An acceptable response

C. A less than acceptable response

The suggested responses:

1 You would explain his role and the extent of his responsibilities and explain how his role and responsibilities fit in with the team overall; you would also say that he should come to speak to you at any time.

2 You would suggest that he goes to see his doctor.

3 You would ask him if there are any changes you could make that would help him feel less stressed and apprehensive.

4 You would tell him to snap out of it and pull himself together.

Your answer:

1	2	3	4

Situation 15

> You are following the usual procedure to induct a new member of your team and are surprised to learn that she is dyslexic.

Rate the suggested responses as:

A. The most appropriate response

B. An acceptable response

C. A less than acceptable response

The suggested responses:

1 You would ask her if there were any special requirements that she needed in order to undertake her role and that should she need things organized differently you would do your best to accommodate her needs.

2 You would describe your commitment to equality of opportunity and how you believe in treating everyone the same.

3 You would explain that you are concerned that this will mean that you will have to provide her with a great deal of support.

4 You would ask her if this meant that she would not be able to undertake some tasks to the high standards expected of your department.

Your answer:

1	2	3	4

Situation 16

> Part of your responsibilities includes the management of workers in the staff nursery school, where there is currently a vacancy for a nursery nurse. You meet with the nursery supervisor to sift applicants for the vacant position. One of the applicants is male and the supervisor explains that you should reject his application because she could not leave a male nursery nurse on his own with the children and he could not be allowed to change nappies on his own.

Rate the suggested responses as:

A. The most appropriate response

B. An acceptable response

C. A less than acceptable response

The suggested responses:

1 You would accept the supervisor's advice and reject the applicant.

2 You would suggest that you stop the sift and resume later after you have had a chance to reread the nursery's policy documents and procedures.

3 You would point out that you would first like to obtain guidance from the human resource department that it is an appropriate thing to do in the circumstances.

4 You would refuse to reject the applicant, pointing out that if you did so then it would be on the basis of gender, which you believe would be wrong.

Your answer:

1	2	3	4

Situation 17

> Your newly formed team is responsible for awarding and monitoring a series of national contracts to outside commercial organizations for the delivery of online training services. The project is new and will roll out nationally following a series of pilot projects that have run for six months. Invitations to tender for the national contracts are to be issued in the spring.

Rate the suggested responses as:

A. The most appropriate response

B. An acceptable response

C. A less than acceptable response

The suggested responses:

1 One of the first things you would do is undertake an analysis of the pilot projects.

2 One of the first things you would do is propose outcomes and performance indicators for inclusion in the new contracts.

3 Your first objective would be to ensure good working relations and collaboration between the members of your new team.

4 Your first objective would be to develop and agree a programme of work and its timing, and assign roles and responsibilities.

Your answer:

1	2	3	4

Situation 18

The project that you lead involves supplying schools with air-pollution monitoring equipment. Under the supervision of their science teacher, schoolchildren from participating schools collect air-pollution data for their playground and report the findings to a central database located in your team. The project is primarily educational but in cases where poor air quality is reported you can request a follow-up investigation by the local authority air pollution unit, and if the schoolchildren's findings are collaborated you have funds to support an initiative to reduce traffic, the emissions from nearby farms or industry or household or agricultural fires, depending on which is found to be the source of the poor air quality.

A head teacher from one of the participating schools has written to you claiming that the children at his school are inaccurately recording the readings from the equipment and so brings into question the validity of the study.

Rate the suggested responses as:

A.   The most appropriate response

B.   An acceptable response

C.   A less than acceptable response

The suggested responses:

1 You would instruct a member of staff to remove the school's recordings from the database.

2 You would write to the link member of staff at all the participating schools, notifying them of the head teacher's concerns and providing advice on how best to instruct pupils on taking readings from the instruments.

3 You would reply to the head teacher, offering advice on how the instruments should be read and the readings recorded. You would also arrange for a member of the team to phone a sample of the science teachers at participating schools, to establish if they too are concerned about the accuracy of the recordings.

4 You would write back to the head teacher, saying that the main objective of the project is educational and so the inaccurate records do not in fact question the validity of the project.

Your answer:

1	2	3	4

Situation 19

> Access to your team's work space is via a flight of stairs. They are quite steep and the steps are narrow. You are concerned that someone may slip, especially when descending. Your fears are made worse because the non-slip strip is missing from one of the steps. These strips were fitted by maintenance when you first occupied the building.

Rate the suggested responses as:

A.   The most appropriate response

B.   An acceptable response

C.   A less than acceptable response

The suggested responses:

1 You would report the missing non-slip strip to maintenance.

2 You would display prominent signs at both the top and bottom of the stairs, advising people to take extreme care, and report the step to the maintenance department.

3 You would report the step to maintenance and tell all your staff that they may work from home until the step has been repaired.

4 You would circulate an e-mail warning staff to take care when using the stairs and in particular to be careful on the step with the missing non-slip tread, and report the missing strip to the maintenance department.

Your answer:

1	2	3	4

Situation 20

Your team is responsible for a project to promote health and social services to members of minority groups who traditionally fail to access these services. You encourage people from these groups to use the services by advertising on community radio and in minority-language papers. You and members of your team also meet with community elders and groups and attend minority-community events. After six months the first set of figures produced by the health authority suggest that despite all your team's hard work there has been little or no improvement in the take-up of services. However, the figures relating to the take-up of social services are more encouraging.

Rate the suggested responses as:

A.   The most appropriate response

B.   An acceptable response

C.   A less than acceptable response

The suggested responses:

1 You would work with your team to identify the reasons why your programme of work has failed to increase the take-up of health services and generate suggestions as to how it might be improved.

2 Despite your understandable sense of disappointment you would try to learn why the project had failed to improve the take-up of health services.

3 As a first step you would invite parties from all relevant and interested bodies to a conference and present your programme of work and an analysis of the results and welcome suggestions as to why it failed and how it might be improved.

4 You would deal with the setback by working harder and encouraging your team to work harder in order that you could place more advertisements, organize more meetings and attend more community events.

Your answer:

1	2	3	4

Situation 21

Your project is almost complete and you are justly proud of the fact that almost all the objectives and outcomes have been realized. The project involves consulting employers on their attitudes towards employing recent offenders. The attitude of employers is important because research by the Home Office has shown that recent offenders who find work after a custodial sentence are far less likely to reoffend than those who do not find work.

The finding of your project has led you to conclude that employers are willing to give young offenders a chance with an offer of employment but that older offenders are less likely to be given a chance and offenders who have committed offences of a sexual nature are almost never going to be offered employment and so remain at greatest risk of reoffending.

You are invited to address a group of offenders at one of the organizations you have worked with on the project. The organization specializes in the rehabilitation of sex offenders and you have been asked to discuss with a group of offenders, many of whom will have convictions for sex offences, how they might disclose their criminal record to prospective employers.

Rate the suggested responses as:

A. The most appropriate response

B. An acceptable response

C. A less than acceptable response

The suggested responses:

1 You would suggest to the offenders that they must disclose their convictions but you would explain that some employers will as a result decide not to employ them; and if they have convictions for sex offences, they may find that the vast majority of employers refuse them employment.

2 You would suggest to the offenders with convictions for sex offences that they should not apply for work as they would have to disclose their convictions and they would find that the vast majority of employers refuse them employment.

3 You would suggest to the offenders with convictions for sex offences that they disclose their convictions only if asked.

4 You would suggest to the offenders with convictions for sex offences that they do not disclose their criminal convictions to employers as if they do so they are very unlikely to be offered employment.

Your answer:

1	2	3	4

Situation 22

You received a complaint regarding one of your staff who with a colleague attended a meeting as a representative of your project. The complaint was from an elected member of the local council, who complained that your team member had implied that it was acceptable for a civil servant to lie. You were very surprised that the complaint was directed towards the particular member of staff because you could not imagine a more honest and truthful civil servant.

Rate the suggested responses as:

A. The most appropriate response

B. An acceptable response

C. A less than acceptable response

The suggested responses:

1 You would reply to the elected representative explaining that your member of staff could not have implied that it was acceptable for a civil servant to lie and there must be some sort of misunderstanding.

2 You would immediately consult with the member of staff concerned and ask if she recalled the incident that had given rise to the complaint. If she confirmed that she had not implied it was acceptable for a civil servant to lie, then you would write to the elected member providing your team member's version of events.

3 You would reply to the elected representative offering an unreserved apology for what must have been a misunderstanding because you know the person concerned to be an honest and truthful person.

4 You would interview both members of your team who attended the meeting and if they confirmed that no one had implied it was acceptable for a civil servant to lie, then you would write to the elected member explaining that you have investigated the complaint and have found that no one had implied it was acceptable for a civil servant to lie.

Your answer:

1	2	3	4

Situation 23

You reported to your line manager as usual last thing on a Friday and were pleased to report that the project was progressing well. However, when you arrived at work on Monday, Matha was already at her desk and she immediately began to explain that she had made a terrible error. You put the kettle on and assured her not to worry and to tell you everything. Once you had established what was worrying Matha, you realized that the consequences for the project were serious and required urgent action if they were not to become even more serious.

Rate the suggested responses as:

A.   The most appropriate response

B.   An acceptable response

C.   A less than acceptable response

The suggested responses:

1 You would immediately set about implementing the urgent action and tell your line manager all about the developments and your response to them at the next Friday meeting.

2 You would immediately set about implementing the urgent action and would inform your line manager of developments straight away.

3 You would inform your line manager of the error and its consequences at the next Friday meeting.

4 You would straight away inform your line manager of developments and agree with him the required urgent action.

Your answer:

1	2	3	4

Situation 24

You are really excited about your first day in your dream post. You can't believe your luck in leading a national project of such importance and one that is so topical. You know very well that if you do well in this high-profile role your career could really take off. Your impression of the role is confirmed when a call from a reporter from a national newspaper is put through to you and you are asked to answer some questions and provide comments for an article that will appear in the paper the next morning.

Rate the suggested responses as:

A. The most appropriate response

B. An acceptable response

C. A less than acceptable response

The suggested responses:

1 You would ask the journalist for her telephone number and say that someone will phone her back once you have checked who is the most appropriate person to deal with her request.

2 You would explain that you are new in the post but are happy to provide comments provided that your name does not appear in the article.

3 You would answer the journalist's questions truthfully.

4 You would tell the journalist that you are new in the post and must check what the correct course of action is before you provide any comments.

Your answer:

1	2	3	4

Situation 25

In just less than a week's time a team of auditors from the Treasury will arrive to examine your project.

Rate the suggested responses as:

A. The most appropriate response

B. An acceptable response

C. A less than acceptable response

The suggested responses:

1 You would ask each member of your team to go through their files to ensure everything is present and in order and that any omissions are corrected in time for the audit.

2 You would personally conduct mini-audits to see if your team's files are in order and ensure that any omissions or errors that you find are corrected before the Treasury team arrives.

3 You would arrange for each member of the team to go through a colleague's files to establish that everything is in order and any oversights are corrected prior to the audit.

4 You would do nothing prior to the audit.

Your answer:

1	2	3	4

Situation 26

It is the first day with your new team and you would organize it so that you:

Rate the suggested responses as:

A. The most appropriate response

B. An acceptable response

C. A less than acceptable response

The suggested responses:

1 start with an icebreaker exercise where you and each member of the team takes turns to introduce themselves.

2 meet with the whole team and then meet with each member of the team individually.

3 start with a series of meetings one after the other with each member of the team and ask staff to bring their project files with them to the meeting so that you can go through them with them.

4 spend it alone, reading all the background papers and files.

Your answer:

1	2	3	4

Situation 27

> You find the role in which you are currently working very challenging because it is so boring. Initially you were enthusiastic about the new appointment but the role did not turn out to be what you expected and you feel that your development is being held back because you spend your time undertaking simplistic administrative tasks. In your opinion the role could be undertaken by an administrative officer and does not require someone like yourself in the grade of higher executive officer.

Rate the suggested responses as:

A. The most appropriate response

B. An acceptable response

C. A less than acceptable response

The suggested responses:

1 You would press on regardless and continue to do the best job that you could.

2 You would ask to meet with your line manager and explain to her how you feel.

3 You would wait until your annual review and use that occasion to explain how you feel.

4 You would start looking for another job.

Your answer:

1	2	3	4

Situation 28

The Civil Service has a proud tradition of political independence and serves the government of the day, whoever that may be. For some time you have grown increasingly uneasy about some of the tasks that you have been requested to undertake, which you consider serve party political ends rather than serve the government. You mentioned your concerns to your line manager and she said that you should simply carry out your assigned tasks to the best of your ability and not concern yourself with whether they are right or wrong. Your concern reaches crisis point when you are asked to help draw up a document to criticize the policies of the opposition party, a task that you feel is far too political.

Rate the suggested responses as:

A. The most appropriate response

B. An acceptable response

C. A less than acceptable response

The suggested responses:

1 Write to *The Times*, enclosing confidential papers proving the political nature of the tasks assigned to you.

2 Take your concerns again to your line manager.

3 Consult the staff handbook and follow the guidelines for raising a grievance.

4 Discuss your concerns with your colleagues.

Your answer:

1	2	3	4

Situation 29

> Half the funds spent through your project are obtained from the European Union and a team from Brussels is due to arrive in a few days to review your project and its expenditure of European funds. You are aware that one of your suppliers has not fully complied with the conditions attached to the European funds. You would:

Rate the suggested responses as:

A. The most appropriate response

B. An acceptable response

C. A less than acceptable response

The suggested responses:

1 say nothing and let the team establish the facts for itself.

2 amend the files so that the non-compliance is hidden.

3 ask for a meeting with the managers of the European team as soon as they arrive and disclose the failure to them.

4 contact the supplier and explain that they have not complied fully with the conditions of the funding and they must do everything they can to correct this situation before the team from Brussels arrives.

Your answer:

1	2	3	4

Situation 30

> Everyone in you team is from time to time late for work but one member of your team is persistently late. In every other respect their performance is satisfactory. Their lateness usually amounts to no more than 15 minutes and they are happy to make up the lost time by staying late.
>
> Every time you meet with them to discuss their timekeeping they assure you that it will improve and normally it does but only for a few days before deteriorating and once again they start arriving late for work.

Rate the suggested responses as:

A. The most appropriate response

B. An acceptable response

C. A less than acceptable response

The suggested responses:

1 Provided they continue to make up the time you would allow the lateness to continue.

2 You would suggest that they start work 15 minutes later than everyone else and stay 15 minutes longer in the evening.

3 You would give them one last chance and explain that if the lateness does not stop you will alert the human resources team and then the matter will be out of your hands.

4 You would arrange a meeting with a representative of the human resources team to discuss the issue and you know they will issue a formal written warning advising the individual to improve their timekeeping or face further disciplinary action. If the lateness continues, their employment will be terminated after a further two warnings.

Your answer:

1	2	3	4

Personality questionnaires

These questions examine your personality type and present you with a series of statements that require you to either agree or disagree or agree strongly or disagree strongly.

Many candidates do not take sufficient care or time over these questionnaires and fail to allow themselves enough time to reflect on every question, ensuring that they answer it in a way that supports their application. Always answer the question in the context of how you would act if you were working for the Civil Service in the role for which you are applying.

It is generally best not to make too many responses that suggest you neither agree nor disagree, as this may be taken to mean that you find it difficult to commit yourself or to make up your mind. Another general point worth remembering is that you should avoid too many agree or disagree strongly responses, as this might risk the impression that you have many strongly held opinions.

Be sure that your answers present you in the best possible light. There is no conflict between giving an honest response while making the best impression. It is perfectly reasonable that you should stress some parts of your personality over others in response to your understanding of the organization's culture and preferred way of working.

Be prepared to make a number of responses that you know will not support your application, as to do otherwise would involve making a misleading response. Everyone will answer some questions in a personality questionnaire with low-scoring responses and it is rare for a few low-scoring responses to determine the overall result.

In Chapter 8 explanations are offered of the likely way in which the questions may be interpreted but answers are not given, as how you respond will depend on you and the position in question.

1   I am impulsive and sometimes regret the things I do afterwards.

   A. Agree strongly   B. Agree

   C. Disagree   D. Disagree strongly

                                                   Answer [   ]

2   If I had to classify myself as either emotional or insensitive, then I would choose the former.

   A. Agree strongly   B. Agree

   C. Disagree   D. Disagree strongly

                                                   Answer [   ]

3 I prefer to eat familiar food rather than try something new that I have not eaten before.

A. Agree strongly   B. Agree

C. Disagree   D. Disagree strongly

Answer [   ]

4 It would be wrong to say that I am thin-skinned.

A. Agree strongly   B. Agree

C. Disagree   D. Disagree strongly

Answer [   ]

5 I would rather pursue my hobby on my own than attend a club with others who share the same interest.

A. Agree strongly   B. Agree

C. Disagree   D. Disagree strongly

Answer [   ]

6 I do not believe that a single heartfelt voice can be louder than a crowd's.

A. Agree strongly   B. Agree

C. Disagree   D. Disagree strongly

Answer [   ]

7 People have said that it is hard to get to know me.

A. Agree strongly   B. Agree

C. Disagree   D. Disagree strongly

Answer [   ]

8 I am more practical than compassionate.

A. Agree strongly   B. Agree

C. Disagree   D. Disagree strongly

Answer [   ]

9 I would describe myself as tactful.

A. Agree strongly   B. Agree

C. Disagree   D. Disagree strongly

Answer [   ]

10   The end justifies the means.

A. Agree strongly   B. Agree

C. Disagree   D. Disagree strongly

Answer [   ]

11   Only those qualified should contribute to a debate.

A. Agree strongly   B. Agree

C. Disagree   D. Disagree strongly

Answer [   ]

12   I prefer to leave a fast-changing situation for others to deal with.

A. Agree strongly   B. Agree

C. Disagree   D. Disagree strongly

Answer [   ]

13   On the occasions when I have felt frustrated with others I wished I had not done so.

A. Agree strongly   B. Agree

C. Disagree   D. Disagree strongly

Answer [   ]

14   It is not true that it is best not to tell someone something they do not want to hear.

A. Agree strongly   B. Agree

C. Disagree   D. Disagree strongly

Answer [   ]

15   I would rather have a career in which I felt I could make a difference than one that offered a very large salary.

A. Agree strongly   B. Agree

C. Disagree   D. Disagree strongly

Answer [   ]

16   In an emergency it may not always be possible to be courteous.

A. Agree strongly   B. Agree

C. Disagree   D. Disagree strongly

Answer [   ]

17   I prefer to work in an environment where responsibility rests with people in more senior managerial roles than my own.

A. Agree strongly   B. Agree

C. Disagree   D. Disagree strongly

Answer [   ]

18   I am sometimes so distracted by my private thoughts that I make small mistakes.

A. Agree strongly   B. Agree

C. Disagree   D. Disagree strongly

Answer [   ]

19   Working as a part of a team is more important to me than keeping abreast of the latest developments in policy.

A. Agree strongly   B. Agree

C. Disagree   D. Disagree strongly

Answer [   ]

20   The views of someone with long service should not be considered more important than those of someone who has only recently joined the Civil Service.

A. Agree strongly   B. Agree

C. Disagree   D. Disagree strongly

Answer [   ]

21   I would not find it irritating if I had to interrupt what I was doing to help with something else.

A. Agree strongly   B. Agree

C. Disagree   D. Disagree strongly

Answer [   ]

22   Before I say something I often find myself pausing to check that what I am going to say is the correct thing.

A. Agree strongly   B. Agree

C. Disagree   D. Disagree strongly

Answer [   ]

23 People would describe my approach to people as bold and decisive rather than delicate and diplomatic.

A. Agree strongly   B. Agree

C. Disagree   D. Disagree strongly

Answer

24 A compromise is rarely the right decision.

A. Agree strongly   B. Agree

C. Disagree   D. Disagree strongly

Answer

25 People who know me would describe my approach as more down to earth than matter of fact.

A. Agree strongly   B. Agree

C. Disagree   D. Disagree strongly

Answer

26 I pay attention to people's motives as to why they say something.

A. Agree strongly   B. Agree

C. Disagree   D. Disagree strongly

Answer

27 My ability to work to a high standard would not suffer if I were in a role that required me to undertake the same task over and over again.

A. Agree strongly   B. Agree

C. Disagree   D. Disagree strongly

Answer

28 It is true that we should all try not to say one thing and do another but in reality at work we sometimes have to.

A. Agree strongly   B. Agree

C. Disagree   D. Disagree strongly

Answer

29   People would say I am sometimes naïve but not wary.

A. Agree strongly   B. Agree

C. Disagree   D. Disagree strongly

Answer [   ]

30   I would rather people described me as approachable than polite.

A. Agree strongly   B. Agree

C. Disagree   D. Disagree strongly

Answer [   ]

Attitudinal tests

In a personality questionnaire it would be very unlikely that a single negative response would result in the failure of your application. However, in an attitudinal test a single negative response could result in the rejection of your application. Take the first example question below. If you could not agree to follow the equal opportunities policy of the Civil Service, then your application would be failed no matter how strong a candidate you were in other respects.

The Civil Service and a host of other employers use this type of questionnaire to try to predict how an applicant once employed might conduct themselves in the workplace. In this context the Service is trying to identify the potential employee who might have the wrong approach to, for example, health and safety, equal opportunities, the handling of a grievance, or the staff whom they manage.

In your current employment you will have a contract of employment and a number of policy documents that form a part of that contract. To help you prepare for an attitudinal questionnaire, reread these documents, as they will help you understand the responsibilities of an employee and what is reasonable for an employer to expect of you. For example, the grievance procedure should state that you should inform your line manager at the first opportunity of something you are unhappy about. The equal opportunities policy will describe how every employee can expect to work in an environment free from the fear of discrimination on the grounds of race, gender or disability. The health and safety policy will require every employee to report immediately anything they consider to represent a danger.

It may well be useful if you undertake an internet search and read up on, for example, what is meant by equality and the value of diversity. Use the following example questions to practice how you will respond in a real test of this sort. Approach each question from the employer's perspective and ask yourself which response would best present you as a suitable employee. By using this approach, together with the suggested background reading, you should find this sort of questionnaire straightforward and you should be able to identify loud and clear the response that the employer is seeking.

Below you will find 30 practice attitudinal test questions.

1   I would not be able to work according to every aspect of the equal opportunities policy of the Civil Service.

A. This is particularly true about me.

B. This is not particularly true about me.

C. Generally this is true about me.

D. Generally this is not true about me.

Answer [   ]

2   The only reason I do not steal is because I would not want others to steal from me.

A. This is particularly true about me.

B. This is not particularly true about me.

C. Generally this is true about me.

D. Generally this is not true about me.

Answer [   ]

3   I do not believe that people in their sixties are not able to adjust to change as well as younger employees.

A. This is particularly true about me.

B. This is not particularly true about me.

C. Generally this is true about me.

D. Generally this is not true about me.

Answer [   ]

4   I believe that a person who can't speak English can expect the same level of service as someone who can.

A. This is particularly true about me.

B. This is not particularly true about me.

C. Generally this is true about me.

D. Generally this is not true about me.

Answer [   ]

5   If your staff were finding it difficult to cope under very stressful working conditions, you would allow them to let off steam by using bad language so long as it was not in the presence of clients.

A. This is particularly true about me.

B. This is not particularly true about me.

C. Generally this is true about me.

D. Generally this is not true about me.

Answer

6   If after leaving a shop I realized I was given too much change I would not turn round, re-enter the shop and point out the mistake.

A. This is particularly true about me.

B. This is not particularly true about me.

C. Generally this is true about me.

D. Generally this is not true about me.

Answer

7   If someone was very rude to me I would show my disdain but nothing more.

A. This is particularly true about me.

B. This is not particularly true about me.

C. Generally this is true about me.

D. Generally this is not true about me.

Answer

8   An extremely challenging client has arrived at reception. He visits the office every few days and is offensive and sometimes threatens violence, although he has never carried out these threats. You know from his casework that he suffers from mental health problems. If you heard one of your staff being disrespectful to the client you might be tempted to make an exception and not reprimand the individual for their inappropriate response.

A. This is particularly true about me.

B. This is not particularly true about me.

C. Generally this is true about me.

D. Generally this is not true about me.

Answer

9 At some time or another everyone makes a mistake and when I make one I try my hardest to put right the situation and then tell the person I report to what happened and what I did to put it right.

A. This is particularly true about me.

B. This is not particularly true about me.

C. Generally this is true about me.

D. Generally this is not true about me.

Answer

10 If I was already very busy and was asked to complete an additional lengthy task I would take it on without complaint or comment. As soon as I have completed what I was already doing I would then turn to the new task and complete it as soon as I was able.

A. This is particularly true about me.

B. This is not particularly true about me.

C. Generally this is true about me.

D. Generally this is not true about me.

Answer

11 In a few very rare circumstances I might make a racist remark.

A. This is particularly true about me.

B. This is not particularly true about me.

C. Generally this is true about me.

D. Generally this is not true about me.

Answer

12 If you heard a colleague being teased about their sexuality you would let people know that you did not think that such comments were appropriate and that they should apologize.

A. This is particularly true about me.

B. This is not particularly true about me.

C. Generally this is true about me.

D. Generally this is not true about me.

Answer

13   I would be OK about someone taking some paper and the odd pen from the office for, for example, a relative's or their neighbour's children and I would not really count this as stealing.

A. This is particularly true about me.

B. This is not particularly true about me.

C. Generally this is true about me.

D. Generally this is not true about me.

Answer

14   I don't agree that my actions speak loader than my words.

A. This is particularly true about me.

B. This is not particularly true about me.

C. Generally this is true about me.

D. Generally this is not true about me.

Answer

15   If I overheard a colleague telling a racist joke I would pretend I did not hear it.

A. This is particularly true about me.

B. This is not particularly true about me.

C. Generally this is true about me.

D. Generally this is not true about me.

Answer

16   I work best when I have to follow clearly defined regulatory procedures.

A. This is particularly true about me.

B. This is not particularly true about me.

C. Generally this is true about me.

D. Generally this is not true about me.

Answer

17   I know that if there is an attractive woman in the team, then it is only natural that any men present will try to impress her.

A. This is particularly true about me.

B. This is not particularly true about me.

C. Generally this is true about me.

D. Generally this is not true about me.

Answer

18 I believe that it is never clever to make a derisory remark.

    A. This is particularly true about me.

    B. This is not particularly true about me.

    C. Generally this is true about me.

    D. Generally this is not true about me.

Answer [＿＿＿＿＿]

19 If you were late for work you would only record the fact in the staff time sheets if you had been seen arriving late by another member of staff.

    A. This is particularly true about me.

    B. This is not particularly true about me.

    C. Generally this is true about me.

    D. Generally this is not true about me.

Answer [＿＿＿＿＿]

20 I believe that women are better at some jobs than men.

    A. This is particularly true about me.

    B. This is not particularly true about me.

    C. Generally this is true about me.

    D. Generally this is not true about me.

Answer [＿＿＿＿＿]

21 I believe that if I have an alcoholic drink in my own time it is not something that my employer should be concerned about.

    A. This is particularly true about me.

    B. This is not particularly true about me.

    C. Generally this is true about me.

    D. Generally this is not true about me.

Answer [＿＿＿＿＿]

22 I just know there are some people I will not get on with.

    A. This is particularly true about me.

    B. This is not particularly true about me.

    C. Generally this is true about me.

    D. Generally this is not true about me.

Answer [＿＿＿＿＿]

23 I believe that you sometimes have to confront aggressive people by being equally aggressive.

A. This is particularly true about me.

B. This is not particularly true about me.

C. Generally this is true about me.

D. Generally this is not true about me.

Answer

24 I would not find it even slightly irritating if I held out my hand to someone and they declined to shake it.

A. This is particularly true about me.

B. This is not particularly true about me.

C. Generally this is true about me.

D. Generally this is not true about me.

Answer

25 I would get involved if I thought someone was being bullied at work.

A. This is particularly true about me.

B. This is not particularly true about me.

C. Generally this is true about me.

D. Generally this is not true about me.

Answer

26 You sometimes have to raise your voice before the point you are making is properly understood.

A. This is particularly true about me.

B. This is not particularly true about me.

C. Generally this is true about me.

D. Generally this is not true about me.

Answer

27 Some people can't take a joke and I think that they would fit in at work better if they lightened up a bit and did not take everything so seriously.

A. This is particularly true about me.

B. This is not particularly true about me.

C. Generally this is true about me.

D. Generally this is not true about me.

Answer [   ]

28 I sometimes find it hard to control my temper but I always manage to.

A. This is particularly true about me.

B. This is not particularly true about me.

C. Generally this is true about me.

D. Generally this is not true about me.

Answer [   ]

29 If someone upsets me, then sooner or later I will get them back.

A. This is particularly true about me.

B. This is not particularly true about me.

C. Generally this is true about me.

D. Generally this is not true about me.

Answer [   ]

30 If I was asked to remove my shoes before I entered someone's home. I would rather leave than do as they asked.

A. This is particularly true about me.

B. This is not particularly true about me.

C. Generally this is true about me.

D. Generally this is not true about me.

Answer [   ]

CHAPTER 5

Practice for the Fast Stream

I used this book to successfully navigate through the initial stages of the Fast Stream process.
READER REVIEW

It should be obvious, but let me make it absolutely clear: you will not find everything you need to pass the Fast Stream in this or any other single volume. Success, for many, only follows what amounts to a major commitment. Candidates who pass prepare for each challenge of the application process. They commit many hours to, for example, revising their maths, developing their written style, practising group discussions and improving their interview skills. Very able candidates may fail a stage of the process and yet find the exceptional strength of character to learn from the experience and apply again in the next round. Many succeed only on their third or later attempt.

Over 100 tips and insights into the Fast Stream

There are no hard and fast, sure-fire winning bets when it comes to psychometric tests, and these tips and insights are intended more as food for thought than dos or don'ts. They are intended to inform and raise awareness of key considerations. Use them to tailor your approach to the Fast Stream competition.

General points

- There are many (at least eight) Fast Stream options, including the graduate Fast Stream, GCHQ Cheltenham, economists, statisticians, technology in business and clerks in both Houses of Parliament. This list is not exhaustive.

- You need a minimum of a 2:2 degree to apply and must be a British national (see the Fast Stream website for definitions). Some of the specialist Fast Stream options require a 2:1 degree or above.

- If it's not too late to decide which degree to take in order to maximize your chances of success, then the overall rate of success by degree type suggests your best chances are if you read economics, a mathematical science, a physical science or engineering (source: inferred from the *Fast Stream Report 2005*).

- Generally the examiners are looking at your writing skills, communications skills, numerical skills, interpersonal and analytical skills and decision-making abilities (source: www.faststream.gov.uk).

- The pass mark is no longer a cut-off – where a certain number of top-scoring candidates are accepted depending on the number of places. Instead, a fixed pass mark is likely to be adopted and everyone who achieves it will be offered a place. If many people succeed, then you may have a longer wait before being offered a place.

- At certain points in the process you have to use the very basic calculator that is provided. This has very few features (it does have a squared function); so, for example, all other powers have to be calculated in longhand (eg $1.06 \times 1.06 \times 1.06 \times 1.06 \times 1.06$).

- Your age will not count against you as long as you have several years to go before normal retirement age; in fact, it may count in your favour as your work experience could greatly help you meet the challenge of the selection process and the role.

- The 'fast' in Fast Stream is all about the speed of progress through the Civil Service grades. The starting salary may not be great but it does go up considerably as you progress through the grades.

- Some people come out of the exercise feeling sceptical about the value of the whole process. They complain, for example, that the distinction between many of the suggested answers in the qualifying tests and e-tray exercise is so fine that it is as much a case of luck as judgement that you choose the 'right' answer. The tests do involve drawing fine distinctions, many of which are a question of precise judgement, and it takes a great deal of practice to tune in to the examiners' way of thinking.

- Overall, just under 4 per cent of applicants are recommended for appointment across all Fast Stream schemes (source: *Fast Stream Report 2005*).

- The significant 'sift stages' for the graduate Fast Stream are the online tests, e-tray and assessment centre (the recruitment process to schemes for specialists such as economists and statisticians may not have all these stages).

- The first part of the application process is online and consists of a self-assessment, application and battery of online tests. Take great care over your presentation and remember that many organizations will reject applications with typos out of hand, so go to the trouble of ensuring that your application is without error. When providing details of your past, check that the dates are correct for both month and year.

  Ensure that addresses, names and titles are complete and 100 per cent accurate. Do not rely on your memory but, for example, go and get the certificates and copy the exact wording, grades and dates.

- You have to register online to begin your application, and will receive a password to access your personal timetable and inbox detailing the stage of your application, details of when you need to have completed stages of the process, invitations to attend events and, perhaps most importantly, results. At www.faststream.gov.uk they ask that you check both your timetable and inbox regularly.

- Once you are through the first stage of the process your qualifications count for very little. What matters is only how well you do in the various stages of the recruitment process.

The qualifying tests

- In the numerical paper, expect a series of questions that follow economic or social numerical data presented as tables, pie charts or bar charts. In the verbal paper, expect a series of passages followed by questions.

- If the last time you revised your mental arithmetic was when you were preparing for your GCSEs, then do not be at all surprised if you do badly.

- In the numerical paper you do get to use a calculator. Even so, if you take the test when your mental arithmetic is not really sharp, then you will probably fail.

- You will find free practice online tests at, for example, www.shl.com and www.psl.co.uk. A word of caution, however: many people complain that the Fast

Stream questions are much harder than the material found on these sites. Still, they may help to get you started (you have to register).

- All parts of the service use the online tests, although there will be different pass marks for the various Fast Stream options.

- The tests have been simplified considerably since the last edition of this book and now rely on only two question types: data interpretation and verbal reasoning.

- The online tests have largely remained the same for the last two years (at the time of going to print).

- The online practice tests mentioned above are very much like the actual tests (though obviously the questions are different), though they have slightly fewer questions than the real ones.

- To make the most of your preparation, first use the questions in this volume, decide which type represents the greatest challenge and then undertake more extensive practice if necessary. Then, when you are ready, take the online practice tests and real tests.

The numerical tests

- The numerical test is approximately 25 minutes long and comprises around 20 questions.

- You are presented with tables, graphs or charts and asked four questions about each. Expect therefore five charts/graphs for 20 questions.

- Candidates with good mathematical skills say they find the numerical test straightforward and complete it in the time allowed.

The verbal tests

- The verbal test comprises around 40 questions to be completed in about 20 minutes.

- You are presented with a series of paragraphs and have to answer five questions about each. The subjects of the individual paragraphs are often slanted towards business but other subjects are also covered.

- The questions are first and foremost about making judgements.

- It can be extremely difficult to identify the right answers from the list of possible options. As mentioned earlier, there are often very fine distinctions to be made. Some candidates find this irritating and hard to accept when compared with the certainty of the numerical test, but you just have to practise to bring your judgement in line with that of the question setters.

- High-scoring candidates complete the tests on time and with a couple of minutes spare to go back and recheck.

- Candidates who have obtained high scores have adopted the following approach: read the passage twice and then reread the relevant bit for each question.

E-tray

Thanks very much for your advice about the e-tray – it was definitely a critical factor in my success.
READER REVIEW

- If you pass the online qualifying tests, then you are invited to attend the e-tray exercise.

- Take this next stage in the process very seriously, as a large number of candidates fail it.

- You may not have come across anything quite like it before, so take time before attempting the exercise to get familiar with the challenge and to develop your approach.

- The practice e-tray exercise on www.faststream.gov.uk does not provide answers, so it is quite hard to know if you are approaching the task correctly.

- The Fast Stream e-tray is split into three parts. We will now look at each in turn.

Part 1 of the e-tray exercise

- In the first part you must read background material. This is likely to include financial information, press articles, academic studies and personnel details of colleagues.

- It is provided onscreen.

- Many people find the time allowed to read all the background material extremely tight.

- Many people come unstuck in Part 1 because they try to take detailed notes. They either find they do not cover all the material, or rush and then cannot decipher their notes later.

- Because of the tight time constraints, rather than trying to take extensive notes you should try indexing the documents so that you can refer back to them when answering questions.

Part 2 of the e-tray exercise

- In the second stage you face an 'inbox' containing 'e-mails', some with attachments.

- Each e-mail is in effect a test question.

- Once you answer one you move on to the next, but cannot return to your previous answer.

- As you progress through the e-mails more arrive.

- This second set of e-mails may be computer adaptive; in other words, their content depends on the answer you gave to the first e-mail.

- The e-mails will relate to a host of issues, including, for example, points of administration, planning or budgeting, and responses to external bodies, other departments and members of the general public.

- You can and should refer to the background papers to decide your response.

- The e-mails may contain attachments that you should read.

- Because you cannot go back to your previously answered e-mails, time management is critical.

- If you get your timing wrong you may, for example, rush through the e-mails and then find yourself sitting with time to spare having finished the exercise. This is almost bound to mean that you have not spent sufficient time on checking the detail of your answers.

- Some candidates find Part 2 of the e-tray exercise to be less time pressured than Part 1.

- In the real exercise, when e-mails start to arrive, you need to refer to the background papers and any attachments to the e-mails to decide on your response.

- When selecting appropriate responses, take care not to overstep your authority by, for example, entering into binding or implied commitments.

- Different questions will test various capacities. These include: how well you can find your way through the background papers, how good you are at prioritizing, how well you can infer from and apply the information to new situations.

- Make sure you demonstrate the sort of qualities that would make a fantastic Fast Stream candidate: for example, balance, integrity, diligence, diplomacy.

- Be especially diplomatic in your handling of the press, outside agencies and other departments.

- Practise writing executive summaries. Do this by abridging articles to two paragraphs or full reports down to two pages.

- It may well help to practise plenty of reading comprehension exercises and critical reasoning tests. Also visit government departments' websites and read as many papers and reports as possible.

- The importance of factual accuracy and attention to detail cannot be overstated. Make sure you get the facts right by referring back. Consider checking figures you are given rather than assuming they are right.

- Success really is in the detail, and seemingly minor points can determine the correct answer. So as you read the briefing documents, look out for and recall what might otherwise be innocent, unimportant points of detail. They can really make all the difference when it comes to the e-mail questions.

- In 2006 a bar at the top of the inbox was added telling you how many e-mails you had answered/read and how many were in your inbox. Some candidates describe this as making things considerably easier.

Part 3 of the e-tray exercise

- The third stage of the exercise involves your writing a memo.

- The memo is about the same subject as the background papers and e-mails.

- You should structure your response using the same guidance as the points below on the written assessment.

Assessment centre: general points

- If you pass the e-tray exercise, then you will be invited to attend the assessment centre.

- Take a moment to congratulate yourself. You have succeeded in a process where the number of candidates has been pared down from well over 10,000 to under 1,000.

- Now put aside all self-congratulatory thoughts and get down to some serious work. You still have a significant series of obstacles to overcome. Begin by studying carefully the very detailed guide to the assessment centre found in the secure section of the Fast Stream website.

- The day may well start early, so ensure you arrive in good time. It is very unlikely that you will be admitted if you arrive late.

- It will be a long day and by the end of it you may well be flagging, but first and foremost try to enjoy it – or at least look as if you are!

- The attendees will be divided into groups and each group will undertake the various assignments at different times. For example, you may do the written assignment in the morning, while others do it in the afternoon.

- A self-assessment form at the end of the day could well be part of your assessment – so answer it thoughtfully and be self-critical, especially with respect to how you might improve your performance.

- Dress smartly but comfortably; a formal suit is not necessary but by all means wear one if you wish.

Written assignment

- The written assignment is completed on a PC, so make sure that your keyboard skills are up to scratch.

- The examiners are looking to see how well you can structure an argument and examine a number of options, recommending one. For this reason it is probably best not to use bullet points.

- Consider starting with a summary of what you say and then commit a paragraph to each of the options.

- State your reasons for not selecting each option as well as making it clear why you recommend your preferred selection.

- If appropriate, use illustrations to make your points.

- Rather than quoting from the background information, consider paraphrasing it or restating the passage in your own words.

- Demonstrate your ability at handling numerical information by offering clear, succinct restatements of relevant data in the background information.

- Cite reference sources.

- Be convincing while remaining impartial and objective.

- Adopt an elegant, fluid, readable style.

- Take care to use correct grammar, spellings and punctuation.

Interview

- At the interview you are likely to face a panel of three, one of whom may well be an occupational psychologist, but don't let this bother you. You will find it a normal interview, so treat it as such.

- It's easy to say, but try not to allow nerves to get the better of you. The interviewers are not trying to find fault or catch you out, but to establish your true potential.

- Do read one of the many interview books, such as *Great Answers to Tough Interview Questions* by Martin Yates, published by Kogan Page.

- Prepare for the usual competency questions. If you have done some of the thinking before the interview, this will help you deal with nerves.

- Be sure you are able to adapt your prepared response to reflect and answer follow-up questions.

- A good interview is first and foremost a conversation where there are mostly points of agreement.

- Be sure you have thought about why you want to be a civil servant, what you believe Fast Stream involves and why you have applied to join it.

Group exercise and presentations

- Identify from the background papers plenty of facts and figures to back up your case.

- Don't worry if your position is entirely different from everyone else's. The assessors are interested in how well you can make your case, not what case you are making.

- Do help ensure that everyone has a say and do show decisiveness and leadership qualities, but avoid adopting the role of chair.

- Make lots of eye contact and nod in agreement, but don't shake your head or demonstrate your disagreement through body language.

- Demonstrate that you can listen and have understood the significance of the contribution of others by modifying your position to take account of their comments.

- Consider making explicit reference to how you have modified your case to take into account the contributions of others. You can do this by, for example, offering supportive summaries of their contributions and then adding a further relevant point of your own.

- Set out to make as good a case as you can for the view that you are representing.

- Don't start or get sucked into an argument; in the unlikely event that one occurs, do try to help make peace between the parties.

- Make sure you are enthusiastic, even when discussing what might seem very mundane issues.

- If you do not have sufficient time to read all of the background papers, make absolutely sure you have sufficient evidence to back up what you plan to say. Include plenty of figures.

- Be constructive in your contributions and be supportive of others in your group.

- Keep your contributions to the point. If you refer to something not obviously significant to the discussion, be sure to spell out its relevance.

- Before you attend, review the competencies that are described as key to a successful Fast Stream candidate (see the website) and make sure that your contribution can be judged as representative of them.

- Be creative, but remember to back up all your points with facts and figures from the background material.

If you get in...

- There are lots of really interesting Fast Stream jobs and some not so interesting, so take care over selecting your parent department.

- Be sure to take responsibility for your own development. If you find yourself in an undemanding role, ask to be transferred to one in which you will learn more.

- When choosing a position, think about the area of work as well as the department. Select the area that interests you most; it might be, for example, the environment, or European and overseas regional policy, or constitutional or legal affairs, or economics and finance – to name but a few.

- You should not expect to stay in any post for more than 18 months.

If, like many, many others, you fail...

- Really very accomplished candidates fail the Fast Stream selection process, so do not conclude that you are not capable of being a very good civil servant.

- Don't be put off. It is common for people to pass only at their third attempt or later. So plan a programme of revision, get down to some serious practice and apply again!

- Taking and failing the Fast Stream is the best possible practice you can obtain! So long as you remain as determined as before, you will definitely do better the next time.

- Sit down and write down your recollection of the process, and undertake some self-assessment of your performance. In particular, reflect honestly on how you might do better next time.

- Use the official feedback, which will give some indication of where you need to improve. Don't expect too much, though; many people are disappointed with its lack of detail.

- This feedback will be computer generated and restricted to broad areas of competency such as handling data and ideas, and working with colleagues.

- There are many other worthwhile entry points into the public sector and structured career paths. Many people, especially graduates, would benefit from realizing that the Fast Stream is not the only route into the Civil Service.

- Departments such as HM Revenue & Customs, HM Treasury and The Highways Agency run their own graduate recruitment schemes. There are also professional entry routes for many disciplines.

- If you join the Civil Service at a non-Fast Stream grade, after two years' service and with your manager's support, you can apply for the 'In-Service Fast Stream'. This is the accelerated promotion scheme designed for those who are already civil servants.

- The overall success rate for the In-Service Fast Stream is almost 50 per cent (source: *Fast Stream Report 2005*).

- Consider reapplying after a few years' work in the private sector. You may well then succeed, as that experience will have helped develop many of the skills tested in the Fast Stream.

Practice for the Fast Stream

The competition is fierce. The Fast Stream usually attracts over 10,000 applicants a year and under 300 appointments are made. To succeed you will have to be very well prepared. If you are serious about wanting to join the programme, set about a significant timetable of preparation. Be prepared to concentrate on the areas in which you do least well. The assessors are looking for both a high score and a well-balanced score. To have any chance of success you have to score consistently well across all the criteria.

The bulk of the material in this and the next chapter is intended to provide practice material for the online tests. The data-interpretation exercises will also help in preparing for the e-tray exercise. This chapter concludes with some exercises to help prepare for the assessment day.

The Fast Stream recruitment process is carefully explained on the website www. faststream.gov.uk. It is vital that you study this site fully and ensure that you are totally familiar with the competencies tested and the nature of each challenge in the process. The Fast Stream is an intense competition and a major test of endurance. You will attempt a series of assessments, often against strict time constraints, over a number of hours. You really have to apply yourself if you are to show your true potential. When you have completed each assessment you should feel worn out; otherwise you cannot expect to stand out from the crowd.

The Fast Stream online tests

This section and the next chapter are intended to provide additional practice questions to supplement those available on the Fast Stream website. Further material is available in other Kogan Page publications including:

The Graduate Psychometric Test Workbook;

How to Pass Graduate Psychometric Tests;

How to Pass Advanced Numeracy Tests;

The Advanced Numeracy Tests Workbook;

How to Pass Advanced Verbal Reasoning Tests.

Ensure that you provide answers to all the questions in both of the online sub-tests. If you do not know the answer to a question, then eliminate as many incorrect answers as you can and then guess.

Warm-up questions for the data-interpretation test

In the real test you have 25 minutes to complete a block of 20 questions.

The test comprises tables of data or passages of information, each of which has associated questions. Five alternative answers are given, from which you must select the right one. Indicate your answer by writing the letter of the correct answer in the answer box.

It sometimes helps to look at the suggested answers before you attempt lengthy calculations, as you may be able to rule out some of the options and then estimate the correct answer by rounding sums up or down to more convenient figures.

Try the 30 practice questions below. Do not use a calculator. Aim to complete them in 25 minutes.

Data-interpretation test

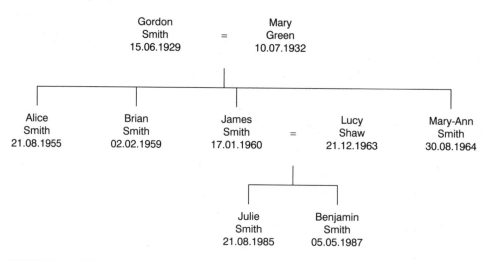

FIGURE 5.1   The Smith family tree

1   How old will Brian be on 01.02.2004?

A. 44	B. 45	C. 46
D. 47	E. 48	F. 49

Answer _____

2   What is the age difference between Alice and Julie?

A. 21 years	B. 25 years	C. 26 years
D. 30 years	E. 32 years	F. 34 years

Answer _____

3   Gordon died in an accident before Mary-Ann was born. Alice was only eight, Brian and James were both four. When did he die?

A. August 1963   B. October 1963   C. November 1963

D. January 1964   E. May 1964   F. June 1964

Answer [   ]

4   Julie and Alice share the same birthday. For presents one year Alice gives Julie a cheque and Julie presents her aunt with a bouquet of roses worth £15.00. Julie quickly calculates that her aunt has spent 25 per cent more than she received. How much money did Julie gain?

A. £2.50   B. £5.00   C. £10.00

D. £15.00   E. £17.50   F. £20.00

Answer [   ]

TABLE 5.1   Top 20 earners, 2001 (averaged across the whole of each profession)

Rank	Occupation	Salary 2001 (£)	Salary 1991 (£)
1	General managers (large companies)	110,341	52,449
2	Barristers	78,549	30,813
3	Senior general administrators, Civil Service	61,993	39,944
4	Treasurers and company financial managers	59,121	25,692
5	Aircraft pilots	57,328	42,055
6	Managers in mining and energy industries	48,916	32,017
7	Doctors	48,235	30,822
8	Insurance underwriters, claims assessors	46,034	28,928
9	Management consultants	45,313	29,914
10	Judges and court officers	45,022	28,435
11	IT managers	43,268	27,440
12	Work study managers	42,867	26,099
13	Police officers (inspector and above)	41,984	30,660
14	Chemical engineers	40,926	26,657
15	Air, commodity and ship brokers	40,421	33,144
16	Solicitors	39,775	28,081
17	Marketing and sales managers	39,750	25,692
18	Personnel managers	37,216	25,187
19	Physicists, geologists and meteorologists	36,829	25,890
20	Air traffic planners and controllers	36,797	27,476

5   Which occupation showed the lowest percentage change between 1991 and 2001?

  A. Senior general administrators, Civil Service

  B. Aircraft pilots

  C. Doctors

  D. Police officers (inspector and above)

  E. Air, commodity and ship brokers

  F. Air traffic planners and controllers

Answer [   ]

6   What is the difference in average earnings between 1991 and 2001?

  A. £14,961.50   B. £15,649.10   C. £16,591.40

  D. £16,914.50   E. £19,164.50   F. £19,654.10

Answer [   ]

7   By what minimum percentage would air traffic planners and controllers have had to increase their 1991 wage to become top of the list in 2001?

  A. 151.1%   B. 199.9%   C. 252.4%

  D. 301.6%   E. 355.3%   F. 410.8%

Answer [   ]

8   Professional athletes earned £17,652 in 1991. If their earnings had increased by 166.3 per cent, where would they have ranked in 2001?

  A. 6th   B. 7th   C. 8th

  D. 9th   E. 10th   F. 11th

Answer [   ]

TABLE 5.2   Gross weekly earnings of full-time adult employees in Great Britain

| | Median gross weekly earnings (£) | | | |
	Manual men	Non-manual men	Manual women	Non-manual women
1986	163.4	219.4	101.1	131.5
1987	173.9	235.7	108.2	142.2
1988	188.0	259.7	115.6	157.1
1989	203.9	285.7	125.9	173.5
1990	221.3	312.1	137.3	191.8
1991	235.4	332.2	147.4	211.1
1992	250.7	353.4	156.6	227.6

9   Which year saw the greatest increase in earnings for manual women workers?

A. 1986–87   B. 1987–88   C. 1988–89

D. 1989–90   E. 1990–91   F. 1991–92

Answer _____

10   How much more must non-manual women workers earn to bring them in line with men in similar occupations in 1992?

A. £23.10   B. £71.00   C. £94.10

D. £102.70   E. £125.80   F. £196.80

Answer _____

11   By what percentage have the earnings of non-manual men workers increased between 1988 and 1992?

A. 36.1%   B. 42.5%   C. 45.6%

D. 49.7%   E. 54.8%   F. 61.1%

Answer _____

12   What was the average weekly wage difference between manual and non-manual men workers between 1986 and 1992?

A. £79.80   B. £80.23   C. £81.40

D. £81.90   E. £82.20   F. £83.60

Answer _____

TABLE 5.3   UK government expenditure on education in real terms, by type

Sector	£ million		
	1970–71	1980–81	1991–92
Schools			
– Nursery	58	114	
– Primary	4,713	5,886	
– Secondary	5,523	7,754	8,287
– Special	442	917	1,280
Higher, further and adult education*	2,884	3,517	3,734
Polytechnics and Colleges Funding Council	–	–	993
Universities	2,325	2,698	2,668
Other education expenditure	706	1,027	1,394
Total	**16,651**	**21,913**	**25,976**
Related education expenditure	2,727	2,678	2,995
VAT on above expenditure	2,132	2,705	5,070
Total expenditure	**21,510**	**27,296**	**34,041**
Total expenditure as a percentage of GDP	5.2	5.5	5.1

* Includes fees for polytechnics and colleges transferred to the Polytechnics and Colleges Funding Council in April 1989.

13   If the fees had not been transferred to the Polytechnics and Colleges Funding Council in April 1989, how much would higher, further and adult education have received in 1991?

A. £993 million   B. £3,734 million   C. £4,727 million

D. £6,401 million   E. £10,135 million   F. £11,128 million

Answer [   ]

14   What was the percentage increase in expenditure on secondary education between 1970 and 1991?

A. 6.9%   B. 40.4%   C. 24.6%

D. 31.3%   E. 45.5%   F. 50.0%

Answer [   ]

15   What was the total GDP for 1991?

A. £34,041 million   B. £58,725 million   C. £509,333 million

D. £568,059 million   E. £667,471 million   F. £680,820 million

Answer [   ]

16 What was the rate of VAT in 1980?

A. 7.5%	B. 11.0%	C. 12.5%
D. 14.0%	E. 15.0%	F. 17.5%

Answer _____

TABLE 5.4 Liverpool tides

Date	High water				Low water				Sun		Moon	
	Morning		Afternoon		Morning		Afternoon		Rise	Set	Rise	Set
	Time	m	Time	m	Time	m	Time	m				
14.04	00:01	9.2	12:16	9.3	06:34	1.1	18:53	1.0	05:30	18:56	19:33	02:29
15.04	00:30	9.1	12:47	9.2	07:07	1.1	19:24	1.1	05:27	18:58	20:46	03:04
16.04	01:00	9.0	13:18	9.0	07:41	1.3	19:56	1.4	05:25	18:59	21:44	03:50
17.04	01:31	8.8	13:50	8.7	08:14	1.6	20:28	1.8	05:23	19:01	22:28	04:50
18.04	02:03	8.5	14:28	8.3	08:48	2.0	21:02	2.3	05:20	19:03	22:59	05:58
19.04	02:42	8.1	15:16	7.9	09:27	2.4	21:44	2.7	05:18	19:05	23:23	07:12
20.04	03:37	7.7	16:24	7.4	10:22	2.8	22:49	3.1	05:16	19:07	23:41	08:26

Table 5.4 shows the high and low tides at Liverpool for one week during April. Information is provided for the time of the tide, its height, and the sun and moon times. Note: all times shown are GMT.

17 What is the range in tide height throughout the week?

A. 1.0 m	B. 7.7 m	C. 8.1 m
D. 8.3 m	E. 9.2 m	F. 9.3 m

Answer _____

18 Which period has the lowest mean tide?

A. morning	B. afternoon	C. both the same
D. cannot be calculated		

Answer _____

19 How many hours of sunlight are there on 17 April?

A. 14 h 38 m	B. 14 h 28 m	C. 14 h 18 m
D. 13 h 78 m	E. 13 h 58 m	F. 13 h 38 m

Answer _____

20 Southport lies 35 minutes behind Liverpool. What time was the morning high tide at Southport on 14 April?

A. There was no morning tide   B. 00:26   C. 00:36
D. 11:26   E. 11:41   F. 12:26

Answer _____

TABLE 5.5 Performance and value of investments

Investment	%	$ value
UK shares	14.6	1,375,200
US shares	9.8	1,976,400
Japanese shares	1.6	406,400
Nickel, silver and gold	62.1	486,300
Crude oil	1.3	2,000,000
UK high risk	(0.9)	700,000
US long term	(0.9)	900,000

Table 5.5 shows the performance of investments in 2006, percentage change on 2005 (in brackets) and $ value of investment at the end of 2006.

21 Find the median percentage change.

A. 87.8   B. 12.5   C. 1.6
D. 1.3   E. –0.9

Answer _____

22 What is the range of the percentage values?

A. 61.2   B. 12.5   C. 62.1
D. 1.3   E. 63

Answer _____

23 Which of the suggested answers most closely represents the increase in value in the investment in Japanese shares since 2005?

A. $6,400   B. $4,064.   C. $6,502.4
D. $4,000   E. $6,000

Answer _____

24 What was the highest sum made on a single investment in 2006?

A. $200,779   B. $193,637   C. $176,400

D. $175,200   E. $174,000

Answer

25 If at the end of 2006 the sum remaining in the UK high risk was moved for a period of three years to a safer investment paying compounded interest at 3 per cent per year, which of the suggested formulas would correctly calculate the sum earned during that term?

A. $693,700 \times 3 \times 3 - 693,700$

B. $700,000 \times (1.03)3$

C. $693,700 \times (1.03)3 - 693,700$

D. $700,000 \times 3 \times 0.3$

E. $693,700 \times (1.03)3$

F. $700,000 \times (1.03)3 - 700,000$

Answer

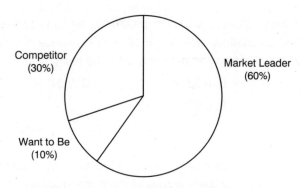

FIGURE 5.2   World market share of all units sold

TABLE 5.6   The business model 2006

Per unit retail price	$9.99
Retailer's commission	$5.49
Cost of sales (per unit):	
Material costs	$1.20
Licence fees	$0.45
Distribution	$0.50
Direct sales team	$0.50
Overheads	$1.50

Figure 5.2 shows the world market shares in sales of the latest 'must have' fashion manufactured by three companies: Market Leader, Competitor and Want to Be. Table 5.6 shows the business model on which all sales are based.

26 Market Leader plans to use its purchasing power to reduce costs and thereby triple the net profit on each unit. This represents what percentage increase over the business model?

A. 100%   B. 200%   C. 300%

D. 400%

Answer [   ]

27 If Want to Be operates according to the business model and sells 2 million units, what net profit would it report (net profit = retail price – all cost of sales)?

A. $7,000   B. $70,000,000   C. $70,000

D. $7,000,000   E. $700,000

Answer [   ]

28 Competitor experiences production problems, and the probability of a unit being faulty is an unacceptable 0.1. Estimate the chance of your buying a unit manufactured by Competitor that turns out to be faulty.

A. 0.02   B. 0.03   C. 0.04

D. 0.05   E. 0.06

Answer [   ]

29 If Want to Be sells 2 million units, which of the suggested answers is the best estimate of the mean for sales across all three manufacturers?

A. 5.5   B. 6.6   C. 7.7

D. 8.8   E. 9.9

Answer [   ]

30 If the business model had existed for four years and the retail price has increased at 5 per cent per annum since then, what was the retail price in 2002 (give your answer to the nearest cent)?

A. $8.25   B. $8.24   C. $8.23

D. $8.22   E. $8.21

Answer [   ]

Warm-up questions for the verbal test

Allow yourself 20 minutes to complete the following 40 questions. They comprise a passage and a group of statements that relate to the passage. Your task is to decide from the information in the passage whether each statement is true or false or whether it is impossible to say. Indicate your answer by writing the letter of the correct answer, A, B or C, in the answer box.

You should avoid relying on your own specialist knowledge or opinions to decide on the answer and rely instead on the information contained in the passage. What this does not mean is that you should be like some Cartesian and start to question every-thing. You need to arrive at a sensible balance and not apply too strict or inflexible a test of proof. It is important that you learn to pick up clues from the wording of the question or statement. If, for example, the question refers to 'a valid inference' or 'a premise', or asks 'Is it necessarily the case...?' then by all means put on your logician's hat and apply strict criteria as to what can be deduced. However, if the question asks, for example, 'Is it reasonable...?' 'On the balance of probability...' 'Might the author...?' then adjust your criterion accordingly and be prepared to apply judgement rather than strict logic.

If you are concerned about this style of question, then take heart from the fact that practice will make a big difference to your approach and performance in such verbal tests. Set aside the necessary time, get hold of sufficient practice questions, and allow yourself to become familiar with the attention to detail and the judgement calls these questions demand. Books on the General Management Attainment Test (GMAT – the test you must pass to get into the world's top graduate business schools) have loads of practice questions of this type.

Practise on the following examples. Remember the advice in tips and insights, that some people find it best to read each passage twice, then reread the relevant part for each question.

Verbal test

Passage 1

An underground railway system is made up of five lines of equal length, all of which run in completely straight lines. The blue line runs north–south and intersects with the red line that runs east–west. The green line runs from southeast to northwest and intersects the red line east of the blue line. The yellow line runs from the northeast and intersects the blue line north of the red line. The grey line runs parallel to the green line, and intersects the blue line south of the red line.

1   The angle between the red line and the blue line at their point of intersection is 90 degrees.

A. True   B. False   C. Impossible to say

Answer [ ]

2   If the grey line were to intersect the red line it would do so west of the green line.

A. True   B. False   C. Impossible to say

Answer [ ]

3   The green line intersects the blue line east of the intersection between the yellow line and the blue line.

A. True   B. False   C. Impossible to say

Answer [ ]

4   The easternmost point of the green line is farther east than the easternmost point of the red line.

A. True   B. False   C. Impossible to say

Answer [ ]

Passage 2

The financial markets are seeking high yields and safe havens, which should boost the Australian and New Zealand dollars, but the Asian currencies have firmed versus the dollar too. Economic growth in East Asia appears to be on a sound footing but the yen's recent strengthening is not regarded as sustainable. Interest rates in the eurozone and UK are unlikely to move for the next few months. These rates are likely to remain unchanged for as much as a year, and then any rise is likely to be small.

5   A rate decrease is expected in the eurozone shortly.

A. True   B. False   C. Impossible to say

Answer [ ]

6   The yen is expected to weaken.

A. True   B. False   C. Impossible to say

Answer [ ]

7   New Zealand's currency will remain aligned with the Australian currency.

A. True   B. False   C. Impossible to say

Answer [   ]

Passage 3

In a league of teams, a win scores two points and a draw scores one point. Team 1 has four more points than Team 2, which has seven fewer points than Team 3. Team 4 has won more games than Team 1 and has lost no games. Team 5, on 17 points, is five points ahead of Team 4. Team 6 has four more points than Team 2. All teams have played the same number of games.

8   Team 4 has more points than Team 1.

A. True   B. False   C. Impossible to say

Answer [   ]

9   Team 6 has more points than Team 3.

A. True   B. False   C. Impossible to say

Answer [   ]

10   Team 2 is bottom of the league.

A. True   B. False   C. Impossible to say

Answer [   ]

Passage 4

The terms 'psychometric tests' and 'psychological testing' are used interchangeably to describe tools that are essentially sophisticated devices designed to measure individual differences in a number of areas such as intelligence and ability. If used appropriately, tests can enhance decision making and enable managers to develop more informed and accurate forecasts of an individual's potential. To achieve this it is essential that the test is integrated into the decision-making process. Even the best tests available are only as good as the process of which they form a part, and flawed decisions can still be made.

11   A psychometric test is the single best predictor of likely job performance.

A. True   B. False   C. Impossible to say

Answer [   ]

12   Psychological tests are most effective as tools to predict individual performance when integrated into the decision-making process.

A. True   B. False   C. Impossible to say

Answer [   ]

13   The principal point of the passage can be summed up as the assertion that
the ability to measure individual differences allows a manager to forecast an
individual's potential.

A. True   B. False   C. Impossible to say

Answer [   ]

Passage 5

During a 14-day holiday that starts on a Sunday, there are three days when the sky
is clear all day. On the 11 days when there is some cloud, it rains on four different
days. On one occasion it rains on consecutive days. On two occasions the sky is
clear all day after it has rained on the day before. It rains on both of the Saturdays,
one Friday and one Wednesday.

14   The days of the week on which it rains consecutively are a Friday and a
Saturday.

A. True   B. False   C. Impossible to say

Answer [   ]

15   The sky is clear on at least one Sunday.

A. True   B. False   C. Impossible to say

Answer [   ]

16   The highest number of consecutive days without rain is six.

A. True   B. False   C. Impossible to say

Answer [   ]

Passage 6

A stakeholder pension plan is a simple and tax-efficient way of saving specifically for
your retirement. All contributions qualify for tax relief at the highest rate you pay, and
growth is free of UK income tax and capital gains tax (the tax on dividends from UK
companies cannot be reclaimed). With a few exceptions, anyone can pay up to
£3,600 gross a year regardless of their age or employment status. Over this level,
further amounts can be invested based on your earnings in the current tax year or

any of the previous five tax years and your age. So, for example, those aged between 46 and 50 years of age can invest up to 25 per cent of their earnings, while those aged up to 35 can invest 17.5 per cent. In general, the older the worker, the greater a percentage they are allowed to invest. Savers can increase or reduce their contributions at any time, or make one-off payments within the overall limits determined by their age and earnings.

17 You will be able to invest more than £3,600 a year into your stakeholder plan if you meet the age requirement.

A. True   B. False   C. Impossible to say

Answer _____

18 Someone who is 27 years of age can invest £5,250 a year of their salary of £30,000.

A. True   B. False   C. Impossible to say

Answer _____

19 If you pay tax at the higher rate of 40 per cent, then your contributions will qualify for 40 per cent tax relief.

A. True   B. False   C. Impossible to say

Answer _____

Passage 7

For sale is an exceptional property overlooking the marketplace, with a triple-aspect reception room commanding views across the popular area. The property is accessed via its own entrance on the ground floor and is arranged over the first, second and third floors of a period property. It comprises approximately 2,000 sq feet of living space. On the second floor are both the bedrooms, of which the master bedroom measures some 18 feet in length. On the third floor is a spectacular open-plan kitchen/family room with a raised dining area and wrought-iron spiral staircase affording access to a roof terrace. Underground parking is available by separate agreement.

20 All the bedrooms are on the floor below the kitchen.

A. True   B. False   C. Impossible to say

Answer _____

21   The reception room is 18 feet in length with commanding views of the market-place.

A. True   B. False   C. Impossible to say

Answer [   ]

22   The reception room is on the first floor.

A. True   B. False   C. Impossible to say

Answer [   ]

Passage 8

The term 'operating environment' refers to the interaction of an information system (typically a computer) with its user. The means of communication between the system, its hardware and software, and the user is called the user interface. The term 'software' can be used to describe both systems software and applications software. The first of these controls the computer's operating systems; the second relates to the user-related programs. The user interface is also called the human–computer interface. Ideally it should be as easy to use as possible, so that the user does not have to study instruction manuals. The interface consists of, for example, cursors, prompts, icons and menus. Prompts can be either visual or audible. Interfaces can be command driven, menu driven or graphical. Command-driven interfaces are fast to use once you have learnt the commands, which are input through a keyboard. Menu-driven interfaces are much more user friendly, and can be input with either a mouse or keyboard.

23   A keyboard is an example of a command interface.

A. True   B. False   C. Impossible to say

Answer [   ]

24   Applications software is user related.

A. True   B. False   C. Impossible to say

Answer [   ]

25   The human–computer interface is a means of communication between the system, its hardware, software and the user.

A. True   B. False   C. Impossible to say

Answer [   ]

Passage 9

Kinematics is the branch of mathematics that deals with the motion of a particle in terms of displacement, velocity and acceleration, without considering the forces that may be required to cause the motion. For motion in a straight line, the distinction between distance and displacement is only that displacement may be positive or negative to indicate direction, whereas distance is always taken as positive. The same point can be made about speed and velocity. Velocity in a straight line may be positive or negative, depending on the direction, whereas speed is always positive. Kinematics can be contrasted with the subject of dynamics, which is concerned with the motion of a particle in response to forces that act on it.

26 Negative values can be used to indicate direction for both velocity and displacement.

A. True   B. False   C. Impossible to say

Answer _____

27 In dynamics speed is always attributed a positive value.

A. True   B. False   C. Impossible to say

Answer _____

28 Kinematics is concerned with the motion of a particle in a straight line but does not concern itself with the forces that act on the particle.

A. True   B. False   C. Impossible to say

Answer _____

Passage 10

A depression is an area of low barometric pressure, which is usually responsible for periods of unsettled weather and often accompanied by strong winds. Depressions occur most frequently in middle and high latitudes. (The most severe storms occur in the low latitudes but these tropical revolving storms must be classified differently from a depression because of the sheer violence they unleash.) Depressions in the northern hemisphere generate winds in an anticlockwise direction, while in the southern hemisphere the winds generated blow in the opposite direction. Most depressions move at speeds of up to 40 miles per hour. They last about three to five days and gradually slow down as the low barometric pressure fills. The wind strengths are reported on synoptic charts by the closeness of the isobar lines: the closer the lines, the stronger the wind strengths. The approach of a depression can be forecast by a fall in barometric pressure and by cloud formations.

29   Someone with a map of the world could establish from the passage that depressions in Australia generate winds in a clockwise direction.

A. True   B. False   C. Impossible to say

Answer [   ]

30   If a depression passes directly over a town, the wind direction shifts through a total of 180 degrees.

A. True   B. False   C. Impossible to say

Answer [   ]

31   If you point your face directly into the wind of a depression in the northern hemisphere, your right ear will point towards the centre of the depression.

A. True   B. False   C. Impossible to say

Answer [   ]

Passage 11

Both sides of a high street are made up of two identical rows of 20 uninterrupted shops exactly opposite each other. There is only one example of each type of shop. Between the pharmacist and the newsagent there are two other shops. Directly across the road from the newsagent is an off-licence. The optician is next door to the insurance broker and two shops away from the off-licence. The pedestrian crossing outside the pharmacist crosses over to the post office, with a clothes shop on one side and butcher on the other. The bus stop is directly across the road from the optician.

32   The pharmacist is on the same side of the road as the insurance broker.

A. True   B. False   C. Impossible to say

Answer [   ]

33   The bus stop is on the same side of the road as the pharmacist.

A. True   B. False   C. Impossible to say

Answer [   ]

34   The optician is next door to the butcher.

A. True   B. False   C. Impossible to say

Answer [   ]

Passage 12

Begin laying the wooden laminate floor in a left-hand corner, with wedges between the boards and the wall, and with the tongues facing into the room. Start the second row with the piece left over from the first row. Leave at least 50 cm between end joints. Apply glue along the whole of the upper side of the groove, on both the long and short sides of the boards. Tap the boards together immediately using a mallet and tapping block. Fit the skirting boards.

35 You would expect the last piece of flooring to be laid in a right-hand corner.

A. True   B. False   C. Impossible to say

Answer [   ]

36 Starting the second row with the leftover piece will help ensure that adjoining end pieces are unaligned.

A. True   B. False   C. Impossible to say

Answer [   ]

37 The short end of the board is its end.

A. True   B. False   C. Impossible to say

Answer [   ]

Passage 13

It takes James nine minutes to get to the meeting, although he sets off five minutes later than Helen. It takes Steve longer to get to the meeting than Helen, but not as long as it takes James. It takes Pete and Sarah the same length of time to get to the meeting, but they do not set off at the same time. Sarah and James do set off at the same time. Steve and Pete arrive at the same time, just after Helen. Richard has to travel further than anyone else.

38 It takes Steve nine minutes to travel to the meeting.

A. True   B. False   C. Impossible to say

Answer [   ]

39 James arrives at the meeting after Helen.

A. True   B. False   C. Impossible to say

Answer [   ]

40   Richard would have to set off before everyone else in order to arrive first.

A. True   B. False   C. Impossible to say

Answer ☐

Recommended source of thousands of further practice questions from the Fast Stream (all found in the Kogan Page testing series):

The Graduate Psychometric Test Workbook;

How to Pass Graduate Psychometric Tests;

How to Pass Advanced Numeracy Tests;

The Advanced Numeracy Tests Workbook;

How to Pass Advanced Verbal Reasoning Tests.

CHAPTER 6

Practice tests for the Fast Stream

This book is excellent preparation for the Civil Service Fast Stream exam.
READER REVIEW

This chapter presents a practice Fast Stream test. As in the case of the real test, there are verbal and numerical sub-tests. The time allowed, number of questions and competencies tested are similar to the online Fast Stream tests. Obviously, unlike the real test, this one is not online – but otherwise treat it as if it were the real thing and take it under test-like conditions. Find a quiet space where you can work uninterrupted. Sit the two sub-tests one after the other, allowing no more than a five-minute break. Try to realize your very best score.

Remember, if you are to show your true potential, you really have to go for it and apply yourself. Make this kind of commitment under practice conditions that simulate the real test. That will help you perfect your exam technique and maximize the benefit of practice.

When you have finished, mark your answers and go over any questions you got wrong.

Do not read too much into your score. This is a practice test, not the real thing, and is intended only as a source of practice. It is not possible to state a definitive pass mark but you should not be content with anything less than a very good score. So make an objective assessment of your performance and set about a programme of revision to address any area of underperformance. If necessary, be prepared to undertake quite a significant programme of revision. Keep practising until you really excel at these sorts of test. You can source hundreds more further practice questions in the books listed in Chapter 5.

Practice test 1 Data interpretation

This test comprises 20 questions. Allow yourself 25 minutes to complete it. Indicate your answer by writing the letter of the correct answer in the answer box.

Be sure to stop as soon as the 25 minutes are over.

You may use a calculator but try not to waste time by relying on it too much. Use one without many functions as this is the sort provided by Fast Stream – then the practice will be more realistic. If you have time to spare at the end of the test, go back over your answers to check that they are correct.

Use rough paper for working out.

Do not start until you are ready to begin.

Data interpretation

Situation 1

Addison, Baldock, Clark, Dickinson, Edwards, Fitch, Gordon, Humphreys, Isaacs, Jordan, Keith, Lloyd, Milton, Newton and Orwell all take extra woodwind lessons on a Tuesday. Using their initials, Mrs Richards, their peripatetic teacher, has produced the monthly timetable shown in Table 6.1.

Each child pays £5.00 per lesson. However, Addison, Dickinson, Edwards, Fitch and Keith are currently subsidized by the school, and pay £2.50. Addison and Edwards will begin paying the full rate from 14 November.

TABLE 6.1   Monthly timetable

Date	5/11	12/11	19/11	26/11
08.30	A	H	F	N
09.00	0	I	K	D
09.30	C	A	H	F
10.00	M	0	I	K
10.30	E	C	A	H
11.00	L	M	0	I
11.30	G	E	C	A
12.00	J	L	M	0
12.30	B	G	E	C
13.00	N	J	L	M
13.30	D	B	G	E
14.00	F	N	J	L
14.30	K	D	B	G
15.00	H	F	N	J
15.30	I	K	D	B

1   On average, which are Mrs Richards's most profitable lessons?

A. 08.30; 09.00; 10.00; 11.00   B. 09.30; 10.00; 12.00; 12.30

C. 11.00; 12.00; 12.30; 13.00   D. 13.30; 14.00; 15.00; 15.30

Answer [   ]

2   When examination time approaches, Mrs Richards offers extra tuition after school at £6.00 per half hour, or £3.50 per pupil if a lesson is shared. Music exams start in December. Clark, Gordon and Humphreys have requested extra lessons. Clark and Gordon both play the saxophone and will share their lesson. Extra tuition starts on 19 November. How much money will Mrs Richards be earning in this week?

A. £75.50   B. £80.50   C. £81.50   D. £83.50

Answer _____

3   Owing to sickness among many of her students, Mrs Richards has to reorganize her timetable for the week of 26 November. The altered lessons are as follows: Edwards at 14.30; Gordon at 10.00; Jordan at 12.00; Keith at 11.00; and Orwell at 13.30. Baldock and Isaacs are away sick. From 13.00 her appointments are as follows:

A. M-A-K-E   B. M-I-K-E   C. M-O-C-K-E-D   D. M-O-L-E

Answer _____

4   The school concert is planned for 22 December. Every student is given five tickets at £4.00 each to sell to friends and family. £212.00 and a number of unsold tickets are returned. Jordan did not sell any, whereas Addison, Dickinson, Fitch, Keith, Lloyd and Newton sold all theirs. What is the average number of tickets sold per student?

A. 2.80   B. 3.00   C. 3.50   D. 4.00

Answer _____

Situation 2

InterSun Ltd has slashed the price of holidays to the Canary Islands. In Table 6.2 its new rates are shown compared with its old fares.

TABLE 6.2 InterSun Ltd holidays

Departure dates		Destination	Board	Price per person/week	
From	To			Old	New
1 July	14 July	Fuerteventura	SC	£150	£125
		Gran Canaria	SC	£165	£130
		Lanzarote	HB	£180	£140
		Tenerife	HB	£200	£150
15 July	28 July	Fuerteventura	SC	£200	£150
		Gran Canaria	SC	£215	£160
		Lanzarote	HB	£230	£180
		Tenerife	HB	£250	£200
29 July	31 August	Fuerteventura	SC	£250	£200
		Gran Canaria	SC	£275	£225
		Lanzarote	HB	£325	£275
		Tenerife	HB	£350	£300

5 A customer wants to visit Lanzarote for two weeks between 7 and 21 July. How much will they save?

A. £80   B. £90   C. £100   D. £110

Answer

6 Airport tax increases on 10 August to £65.00 per person, from an original £42.00 per person. InterSun Ltd has already sold 6,731 holidays for this period and cannot now introduce the new charge to these customers. What are its losses?

A. £154,813   B. £154,956   C. £164,765   D. £165,814

Answer

7 Self-catering holidays offer a further 25 per cent reduction on prices for holidays in Fuerteventura during August. What is the total saving on the original price for a two-week holiday starting on 21 July?

A. £187.50   B. £175.00   C. £160.50   D. £150.00

Answer

8 In August, which destination has the greatest percentage increase over the late July rates?

A. Fuerteventura   B. Gran Canaria   C. Lanzarote   D. Tenerife

Answer

Situation 3

Kash Ltd offers personal loans at 8.9 per cent APR. Table 6.3 shows the repayments over various monthly instalments, either with payment protection cover (PP) or without payment protection cover (W/O) for loans between £5,000 and £20,000. Payment protection cover ensures continued loan repayments in the event of involuntary unemployment, illness or disability. All repayments are fixed for the entire period of the loan and guaranteed never to rise.

TABLE 6.3   Kash Ltd

| Loan | 12 months | | 24 months | | 36 months | | 48 months | | 60 months | |
£	W/O	PP	W/O	PP	W/O	PP	W/O	PP	W/O	PP
20,000	1,745.26	1,865.77	909.97	999.94	632.22	704.25	793.85	569.86	411.23	482.21
17,500	1,527.10	1,632.55	796.22	875.03	553.19	616.22	432.12	498.63	359.83	421.94
15,000	1,308.95	1,399.33	682.48	750.03	474.16	528.19	371.39	427.40	308.42	361.65
12,500	1,090.79	1,166.11	568.73	625.02	395.14	440.16	308.65	356.16	257.02	301.38
10,000	872.63	932.89	454.98	500.01	316.11	352.13	246.92	284.93	205.62	241.11
8,000	698.10	746.30	363.99	400.02	252.89	281.70	197.54	227.95	164.49	192.88
6,000	523.58	559.73	272.99	300.01	189.66	211.27	148.15	170.95	123.37	144.66
5,000	436.32	466.45	227.49	250.01	158.05	176.06	123.46	142.46	102.81	120.55

Note: customers who do not satisfy Kash Ltd's normal scoring criteria may be offered a loan with an APR of up to 4 per cent above the typical rates shown. An additional variable administration fee will also be payable; information concerning that is available upon request.

9 How much will a customer repay Kash Ltd for a loan of £12,500 borrowed over 48 months (with payment protection cover)?

A. £13,676.64   B. £14,815.20   C. £15,421.20

D. £17,095.68   E. £18,505.20   F. £20,515.20

Answer _____

10 Kash Ltd offers a repayment plan of £154.21 over 60 months for a loan of £7,500. This is a saving of £598.80 on a competitor, Loans-R-Us Ltd, which offers its customers an APR of 11.9 per cent over the same period. How much in total do customers of Loans-R-Us Ltd repay?

A. £8,098.80   B. £9,252.60   C. £9,851.40

D. £9,993.50   E. £10,156.00   F. £10,512.80

Answer _____

11 Mr Patel requests a loan of £10,000. Which of the following is his cheapest form of repayment?

A. 12 months PP   B. 24 months W/O   C. 24 months PP

D. 36 months W/O   E. 36 months PP   F. 48 months W/O

Answer [   ]

12 Unfortunately Mr Fox has a very poor credit rating and Kash Ltd has offered him an APR 3 per cent above the typical rate for a loan of £5,000. What are his monthly repayments (without payment protection cover) over 36 months?

A. £164.40   B. £176.06   C. £185.45

D. £187.60   E. £191.23   F. cannot be calculated

Answer [   ]

Situation 4

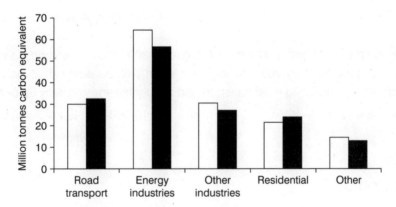

FIGURE 6.1   UK CO$_2$ emissions, 1993 and 2007
Source: DEFRA

Key
Black bars 1993
White bars 2007

Figures
Road transport 1993 30.0 mt; 2007 31.5 mt
Energy industries 1993 63.0 mt; 2007 57.0 mt
Other industries 1993 27.0 mt; 2007 28.9 mt
Residential 1993 22.0 mt; 2007 23.32 mt
Other 1993 12.74 mt; 2007 14.0 mt

13 Which pair of bars saw the greatest percentage increase over the 14-year period?

A. Road transport   B. Energy industries   C. Other industries

D. Residential   E. Other

Answer _____

14 Express in its simplest form the ratio between emissions in 1993 for energy transport and other industries.

A. 5:3   B. 6:3   C. 7:3   D. 8:3

Answer _____

15 If CO_2 emissions from road transport prior to 1993 had increased by 10 per cent per annum, in what year would emissions from road transport have amounted to 20 million tonnes?

A. 1991   B. 1990   C. 1989   D. 1988   E. 1997

Answer _____

16 By what percentage would the UK's overall 2007 CO_2 emissions have fallen if the government's road-pricing and energy-efficient-homes policies had succeeded in cutting road transport and residential emissions by 50 per cent?

A. 0–5%   B. 5–10%   C. 10–15%   D. 15–20%   E. 20–25%

Answer _____

Situation 5

TABLE 6.4 Rate of exchange and percentage change in that rate

Currency	Currency: euro rate yesterday	Today's rate as % change on yesterday
peso	1:0.055	4%
rupiah	1:0.00084	–6%
yuan	1:0.099	8%
balit	1:0.021	–2%
ringgit	1:0.022	?

17 If today's exchange rate for the balit:euro is 1:0.01995, what was the percentage change on yesterday's rate?

A. 5%   B. 3%   C. 1%   D. –3%   E. –5%

Answer _____

18   What is the peso:euro rate today?

A. 1:0.0572   B. 1:0.0563   C. 1:0.0539   D. 1:0.0528

Answer

19   What is today's rate for the rupiah:euro?

A. 1:0.0008904   B. 1:0.0008196   C. 1:0.0007896

D. 1:0.0006986

Answer

20   If issued in response to the change in the rate of the yuan, which statement has most credence, given that economic zones export dependency?

A. The change will fuel inflation within the yuan zone.

B. Outflows of money seeking higher returns are causing the change.

C. The international headlines of mass street protests in the yuan zone are causing the currency's fluctuation.

D. The change will help hold down inflation within the yuan zone.

Answer

End of test.

Practice test 2 Verbal test

This test comprises 40 questions to be completed in 20 minutes. Use it to practise making judgements and correct inferences. Indicate your answer by writing the letter of the correct answer in the answer box.

Be sure to stop as soon as the 20 minutes are over.

Practise the recommended strategy of reading each passage twice and then referring back to the passage to answer the specific point raised in the question. If you have time to spare at the end of the test, go back over your answers to check you are happy with them.

Do not start until you are ready to begin.

Verbal test

Passage 1

Widespread help from parents and family members generally has always cast doubt on the value of examinations in which home-completed assignments contribute to the grade awarded. Between 20 and 60 per cent of marks generally come from such coursework. Most students believe that coursework is a fairer method of assessment when compared with 'all or nothing' exams; however, they also admit that it is 'all too easy to cheat'. A review of the extent of cheating found overwhelming evidence of widespread abuse by students, teachers and parents. Incredibly, 1 in 10 parents admitted to doing assignments for their children. Teachers admitted to giving students 'too much help'. But the greatest concern arises because of the internet. A whole host of sites now exist that offer model essays and examples of coursework awarded top grades for a small fee (or even for free). Most of these sites carry requests that users should not submit the material as their own, but there is no attempt to ensure that this request is respected and there is much evidence of a plagiarism free-for-all of internet-obtained material.

1   In the passage it is concluded that the internet has made the policing of course-work impossible.

    A. True   B. False   C. Cannot tell

                                      Answer [   ]

2   The extent of the contribution from home-completed assignments to the grade awarded can be best described as:

    A. significant   B. serious   C. noteworthy

    D. a scandal   E. insufficient information to answer the question correctly

                                        Answer [   ]

3   The author relies on which one of the following to make his claims?

    A. Examples or analogies

    B. Deductive argument

    C. The drawing of comparative assertions

    D. The findings of a investigative study

    E. The results of an experimental investigation

                                        Answer [   ]

4   It is reasonable to infer from the passage that widespread help from parents and siblings has raised serious questions about the credibility of vocational qualifications.

A. True   B. False   C. Cannot tell

Answer [   ]

Passage 2

A study of the benefits of a family of cholesterol-lowering drugs used in the treatment of heart attacks has shown that while the greatest benefits are enjoyed by those at greatest risk of a vascular event, every person at risk can gain considerable benefits from the treatment. These findings have led to calls that it should be offered to any-body at risk of a heart attack or stroke. It has long been known that the treatment, if administered daily to the group most at risk of an attack, sees that risk cut by a third. At present doctors prescribe the treatment only once they have considered a number of factors, including cholesterol level, blood pressure, body-fat levels and whether the patient smokes. The new evidence suggests that patients with less than very high levels of cholesterol will also experience a significant drop in their cholesterol levels and a consequently lower risk of a vascular event. In fact, the study concludes that the benefits of the treatment are directly proportional to the size of the reduction in cholesterol levels that might be achieved, and not the level at which the intervention begins.

5   A factor that gave rise to the call for the treatment to be offered to everyone at risk of a heart attack or stroke was the realization that not every person at risk can gain considerable benefits from the treatment.

A. True   B. False   C. Cannot tell

Answer [   ]

6   Which of these statements, if true, would most weaken the claim that patients with less than very high levels of cholesterol will also experience a significant drop in their cholesterol levels and a consequent much lower risk of a vascular event?

A. The largest benefits from the treatment are seen among those at greatest risk of a vascular event, and those with less than very high levels of cholesterol are not at greatest risk.

B. Unfortunately, the best results from the treatment can only be obtained when the treatment is customized to the individual patient's cholesterol levels; achieving the optimum effect requires someone with less than very high cholesterol levels to take a smaller daily dose.

C. Preliminary evidence suggests that the treatment achieves a relatively small reduction in the risk of a heart attack among people with less than very high levels of cholesterol.

D. Not all the evidence is positive, as people with lower cholesterol levels who take the treatment have been found to develop an increased risk of some cancers.

E. Originally it was thought that the treatment worked by lowering the cholesterol level, but it is now believed that this effect alone is not enough to account for all the advantages that the treatment provides.

Answer [   ]

7   New evidence suggests that the treatment could cut heart attacks by a third.

A. True   B. False   C. Cannot tell

Answer [   ]

8   Given that the benefits of the treatment are directly proportional to the size of the reduction in cholesterol levels achieved, doctors should look more to the relative drop in cholesterol that may be achieved through the treatment rather than prioritizing patients suffering the very highest levels.

A. True   B. False   C. Cannot tell

Answer [   ]

Passage 3

The projection in the latest quarterly inflation report is for growth to pick up to 2.8 per cent. For this forecast to be realized, household spending and domestic consumption would need to increase noticeably from their current lacklustre levels. The economy has grown at a rate below its long-term trend for three out of the last four quarters. Wage growth was under control and the high-street and housing markets, while not getting worse, were not getting any better either. Import prices had started to add to inflation after years of deflation, in the wake of the $25 jump in the barrel price of crude. But most economists felt it best to ignore the first-round impact of this rise and wait for any domestic secondary effect – higher prices in the shops – before taking action. That action will almost certainly involve interest rate increases, the effect of which would be to squeeze household spending and knock back inflation. The economy would then have to wait for the stable job markets and increases in incomes and wage growth to diminish the effect of the rate increase over the medium term. Eventually these factors would give rise to domestic growth at or above the long-term trend. In the meantime the risk of either a full-scale consumer recession or a collapse in house prices is very slight.

9   The main theme of the passage is the question of whether or not oil-price inflation must lead to higher interest rates.

A. True   B. False   C. Cannot tell

Answer [   ]

10   The author would agree that wage growth and incomes will increase if the job
markets remain steady.

A. True   B. False   C. Cannot tell

Answer [   ]

11   The author does not believe that the economy is on target to realize the projection for growth given in the last quarterly inflation report.

A. True   B. False   C. Cannot tell

Answer [   ]

12   Which of the following statements would the author of the passage most likely
agree with?

A. The wider community of economists is split over whether monetary policy
should pay heed to the immediate price impact from oil.

B. Broadly speaking, economists agree that immediate action should be taken
against the inflationary effects of the $25 jump in the price of crude.

C. The wider community of economists rejects the view that the best monetary
policy is to take no action over the immediate impacts of the oil-price rise.

D. Most economists are for ignoring any rise in non-oil inflation.

E. None of the above.

Answer [   ]

Passage 4

Road congestion has grown by 37 per cent, and as people switch from private cars
to public transport the total distance travelled by rail is expected to increase by 60 per
cent. Despite the obvious increase in demand for space on our roads and trains,
governments are failing to match forecast growth with investment in either mode of
transport. In the 10 worst areas the problems are already chronic, with immediate
investment needed if sufficient capacity is to be created to cope with future demand.
In these areas, new roads and tracks, and longer platforms that can handle longer
trains, are already needed to relieve bottlenecks, congestion and severe overcrowding during peak hours. Despite demand, there are no plans to significantly expand

road and rail networks, and indeed closures and cuts in funding are on the agenda. The paucity of public investment raises considerable doubts as to whether those few projects that are currently supported will ever be completed, because ministers are refusing to say how much public money they will receive.

13 As road congestion has grown, the total distance travelled by rail has increased.

A. True   B. False   C. Cannot tell

Answer [   ]

14 The passage describes the transport infrastructure of northern Europe.

A. True   B. False   C. Cannot tell

Answer [   ]

15 It is hard to arrive at any other conclusion than that travellers face a bleak future of:

A. overcrowded networks, slower journey times and higher fares.

B. congestion, bottlenecks and overcrowding.

C. congestion, overcrowded networks and higher fares.

D. overcrowding, congestion and even slower journey times.

E. slower journey times and higher fares.

Answer [   ]

16 The type of projects that are supported but which may never be completed because of diminutive public investment are:

A. road projects   B. rail projects

C. both road and rail projects   D. not specified

Answer [   ]

Passage 5

The Agency for Crude Oil estimates that China's imports of crude will increase by 8 per cent year on year, a figure more than twice the predicted rate of growth in global demand. To protect Chinese farmers, the group that has gained least from the economic reforms, and to avoid social unrest, the People's Congress has held the price of diesel at the pumps artificially low. These price controls mean that Chinese state-owned refineries are losing vast sums of money when supplying domestic markets. To offset these losses, the refinery managers must export fuel, and this is the single most important cause of the chronic fuel shortages facing the domestic market of China.

China's energy companies are desperately trying to resolve the issue by securing more suppliers of crude. Their greatest hope lies with Russia, which currently only supplies a small fraction of China's annual consumption. Chinese officials would dearly love a pipeline from the Siberian oilfields. But Russia is anxious to keep control of its export market and is understandably reluctant to provide its neighbour's refineries with oil only to see it sold on to a third party in order to cross-subsidize the artificially low cost of fuel on China's domestic markets.

Perhaps a more viable solution lies with a price increase in the cost of diesel in Chinese domestic markets. This might well mean that the current runaway demand will be curtailed and Chinese refineries will be better able to supply their home markets.

17   Which of the following terms is most appropriate in describing the difficulties China is experiencing over the supply and demand of crude oil for its domestic markets?

A. catastrophe   B. tragedy   C. predicament

D. snag   E. complication

Answer [   ]

18   Which of the following is mentioned as a solution to fuel shortages?

A. securing more suppliers of crude

B. a pipeline from the Siberian oilfields

C. an end to refineries selling overseas

D. an end to the artificially low cost of fuel on China's domestic markets

E. curtailment of the current runaway demand

Answer [   ]

19   Which topic is not touched upon in the passage?

A. fiscal policy   B. international relations

C. fuel exports   D. retail price   E. rationing

Answer [   ].

20   China is keeping a lid on prices at the pumps to protect the group that has gained least from the economic reforms.

A. True   B. False   C. Cannot tell

Answer [   ]

Passage 6

We may not much like the fact, but we are 99.9 per cent identical. This is because 99.9 per cent of our DNA is common to every person, and the Human Genome Project is rightly celebrated for sequencing it. But what of the remaining 0.1 per cent? It is far more significant than one might assume, because if it were not for this minute percentage there would be no individual differences. We would be clones. These variations in the human code account for all individual idiosyncrasies. They are responsible for the differences between ethnic and racial groups. Perhaps most interesting of all, they also explain why some of us enjoy good health, while others are more susceptible to many common diseases. It is thought that the mapping of the remaining 0.1 per cent of human DNA will hasten the identification of new ways to treat common ailments such as obesity, cancer and heart disease. The work will prove particularly useful in the search for new diagnostic tests, the customizing of treatments to best suit an individual's genetic code, and ultimately the development of new drugs that target the DNA linked to a particular disease. The task of charting the inherited differences in the human genome has fallen to 200 scientists drawn from nine countries across every populated continent. They will screen people drawn from all the major human populations.

21 Sequencing is only mentioned in the passage in relation to the work of the Human Genome Project.

A. True   B. False   C. Cannot tell

Answer

22 It can be inferred that the work will:

A. accelerate the search for genes involved in common diseases.

B. chart the inherited differences in the human genome.

C. speed up the development of new treatments.

D. map the DNA that is shared by every person.

E. be made freely available on the internet.

Answer

23 The issue of preventative therapies is mentioned.

A. True   B. False   C. Cannot tell

Answer

24 In reaching the conclusion that some of us enjoy good health while others are more susceptible to many common diseases, the author relies on the premise that:

A. humans are 99.9 per cent genetically identical.

B. the genetic differences between people hold the key to our predisposition to many common diseases.

C. just 0.1 per cent of the human genetic code accounts for all the genetic differences between human beings.

D. the human genome sequence provides us with a blueprint of all the DNA shared by every human being.

E. the sequencing of the genetic differences allows scientists to identify genes that influence common diseases.

Answer ⬚

Passage 7

We all know that our criminal system is failing, but how many of us know the extent of the failure? Do you know, for example, that 9 out of 10 offenders reoffend within two years of completing their punishment? Our prisons are so overcrowded that programmes of education and rehabilitation have been abandoned. Offenders rarely get a prison sentence on the occasion of their first conviction. They are far more likely to be sentenced to a curfew monitored by an electronic tag and police surveillance. But by the time they have appeared before the judge on the third or fourth occasion, all hope that community-based punishments will work is abandoned and the persistent offender is sentenced to a period of imprisonment. Of those who are given a curfew order, many don't even wait for the end of the period of curfew before reoffending. Large numbers breach their curfew repeatedly and even remove their electronic tag. Under the current system even the fear of being caught and punished again is failing to deter. No wonder crime rates are soaring.

25 Which of the following statements serves as a premise to the author's main claim?

A. That rehabilitation programmes reduce offending rates.

B. That today's punishments fail to deter reoffending.

C. That the objective of punishment is to deter reoffending.

D. That the frequency of reoffending is increasing.

E. That crime rates are soaring.

Answer ⬚

26 The reason for the abandonment of rehabilitation programmes is that the prisons are so overcrowded that prisoners must forgo education and rehabilitation programmes so that staff may concentrate on issues of security.

A. True   B. False   C. Cannot tell

Answer ☐

27 Which of the following sentences would most likely follow as the next in the passage?

A. It is abundantly clear that we need to find workable alternative solutions to tackle this very real challenge to society.

B. Perhaps we need to find other ways to punish those in society who refuse to stop offending.

C. Persistent offenders need longer sentences that might change their attitude towards rehabilitation programmes and encourage them to reform their criminal behaviour.

D. It seems beyond the wit of everyone involved to find a workable way of curbing the rate of offending by persistent young offenders.

E. Recidivism will decline as long as our community- and prison-based punishments fail to deter the persistent offender.

Answer ☐

28 The criminal system is slow or unwilling to provide the resources required for rehabilitation provision.

A. True   B. False   C. Cannot tell

Answer ☐

Passage 8

We face a pensions crisis because more than half of all working people will rely solely on the state to provide a pension in their old age. These people have paid into a state pension scheme all their working lives. In return they expected to be provided with a state pension on which to live during their old age. Why then the crisis? In the 1960s there was one pensioner for every five workers; this ratio has dropped to one pensioner for every three people in work and is forecast to go as low as one to every two within the next 20 years. The government will simply not be able to provide pensions to the millions of retired people. To make ends meet it is estimated that the government will have to cut the low pension rate by 30 per cent. This means that those who rely solely on the state for a pension may well find themselves retiring to utter poverty.

This will directly affect around 12 million people, so it is no wonder people are talking about a crisis. A large slice of the other half of the working population is also at risk of retiring to poverty. These workers have, as well as their state pension, a private scheme to which they contribute and which they intend to use to top up their state pension in retirement. However, most are contributing only a pittance towards these schemes and have funds currently valued at less than $10,000. On their retirement, most of these people will find that their private schemes are insufficient to buy them a meaningful second source of income.

29   In making his case the author relies on the assumption that the government has not been putting aside workers' contributions so that it can meet its future pension commitments.

A. True   B. False   C. Cannot tell

Answer [   ]

30   The number of people at risk of retiring into poverty is:

A. less than 12 million   B. exactly 12 million

C. around 12 million   D. more than 12 million

Answer [   ]

31   A net influx of migrants would help improve the future pensioner–workers ratio.

A. True   B. False   C. Cannot tell

Answer [   ]

32   Which of the following would most likely follow on as the next sentence in the passage?

A. The government faces an $800 billion bill for public sector pensions.

B. They too will not be able to enjoy a decent quality of life in their retirement.

C. Long-awaited proposals to tackle the looming crisis were rejected out of hand by the government yesterday.

D. They too eagerly await proposals as to how the crisis might be avoided.

E. Long-awaited proposals as to how workers can be encouraged to save more for their retirement were announced recently.

Answer [   ]

Passage 9

The 1707 Act of Union, the legislation that enshrines the constitutional unification of Scotland and England, passed almost without celebration on its tercentenary. The Scottish National Party (the political party that seeks Scottish withdrawal from the union) is set to take control for the first time of the devolved Scottish Parliament. This once again raises the question of how an independent Scotland might prosper. Much is made of North Sea oil revenue, which if allocated entirely to Scotland would this year amount to more than £10 billion. This is by no means a typical year, however, as annual oil revenue has averaged nearer £6 billion. Other tax incomes total something in the region of £30 billion annually. Currently, annual expenditure in Scotland is estimated to be approaching £50 billion. To be more definite after so many years of unification is difficult. In any event, a people of 5 million may well be very willing to chance the consequences of independence and capable of achieving a dynamism that overcomes the cost and potential drawbacks of independence.

33   It is reasonable to infer that the fledgling state of Scotland would:

   A. face a significant fiscal deficit.

   B. enjoy an enviable monetary surplus.

   C. face some hard choices.

   D. be able to revive its fortunes.

   Answer [   ]

34   The author would agree with the assertion that Scotland could afford independence.

   A. True   B. False   C. Cannot tell

   Answer [   ]

35   It can be surmised that the state of the economy of an independent Scotland would be:

   A. in no time at all as successful as the Republic of Ireland.

   B. less dependent on shifts in the world's crude oil markets.

   C. comparable to that of Sweden.

   D. more dependent on price fluctuations in the price of its crude oil.

   Answer [   ]

36 In any split from the United Kingdom of Great Britain and Northern Ireland, Scotland is unlikely to be allocated the entire proceeds from North Sea oil.

A. True   B. False   C. Cannot tell

Answer [   ]

Passage 10

Since 1997 over 1 million children have seen their family's income rise to the point where they are no longer defined as being in poverty. This has been achieved through an increase in levels of employment and the minimum wage, and increases in the level of state benefits paid to families. Despite these gains, marital break-up, youth unemployment, teenage pregnancy and violent crime committed by young people are all at record high levels. Opponents argue that undeniably greater prosperity has failed to lead to greater social cohesion. As the principal cause, they point to the current policies' failure to support the institution of marriage. Fiscal policy, since the abolition of the married couples allowance and the introduction of family tax credits, offers no recognition of marriage. Whatever opponents propose, it is likely to include a far greater emphasis on the family unit as one that comprises a married couple, both of whom are living with their children. These opponents make it clear that their proposals will equally apply to gay couples caring for children and living in civil partnerships.

37 Youth unemployment is higher than in 1997.

A. True   B. False   C. Cannot tell

Answer [   ]

38 It is reasonable to infer from the passage that an important difference between these two points of view comes down to the definition of the family. The opponents to current policy view it as comprising:

A. a couple who live with their children.

B. a married man and woman cohabiting with their children.

C. a gay couple with parental responsibilities who have made a commitment through a civil partnership.

D. an unmarried woman with children.

E. None of the above.

Answer [   ]

39 The abolition of the married couples allowance occurred in 1997.

A. True   B. False   · C. Cannot tell

Answer

40 The opponents' family agenda is directed against:

A. single mothers   B. absent fathers

C. social cohesion   D. social ills

Answer

End of test.

CHAPTER 7

Preparing for the assessment centre

If you receive an invitation to the assessment centre, then you have made it through to something like the thousand candidates (across the combined Fast Stream options) and you should feel justly content. You should also appreciate that you are soon to be subjected to an entirely different sort of assessment to the one so far. This is because now that the numbers are more manageable, the service will start examining you more as an individual rather than a statistic.

At the assessment day it is essential that you present yourself as a candidate fit for the Fast Stream. Attend with the intention of making every word you say or write sound like one uttered or written by the perfect Fast Streamer.

Start your preparations early and start by reflecting on the competencies and qualities that make an ideal Fast Stream candidate. You will find a description of the qualities at various points on the Fast Stream website. You need to explore the meaning of these descriptions and build up your own impression of the qualities the ideal candidate would portray.

To help get you thinking and build your impression of the ideal candidate, consider the following list of qualities and prioritize them in terms of whether you consider they are essential or desirable for the role. They are not from any official source, nor are they a complete list of the competencies a Fast Streamer should possess, just some issues it might help to think over.

Once you have formed a view of the qualities held by the ideal Fast Streamer, set about making sure that an assessor will attribute these qualities to you. Do this by:

- making sure that you can illustrate a time when you have portrayed each of the qualities, and use these to inform your responses in the interview;

- reflecting on how you might conduct yourself in a group exercise so that an assessor might attribute these qualities to you;

- devising some broad strategies that are characteristic of these competencies and work out how you might adopt them in a written assessment.

The qualities to think about are:

- Analyse problems in a logical and well-organized way.

- Cooperatively develop practical solutions to problems.

- Show clarity of vision in the assessment of intricate circumstances.

- Provide clear direction in the management of change.

- Identify appropriate principal goal(s) for a complex assignment.

- Assign and communicate roles to each member of a team.

- Offer compelling arguments.

- Interact creatively and positively with colleagues and representatives of outside organizations.

- Show diplomacy, integrity and diligence.

- Anticipate through suitable strategies future trends, problems or opportunities.

- Win support for new initiatives.

● Negotiate effectively with representatives from a broad church of interests, backgrounds and groups.

```
```

● Demonstrate a mastery of numerical data.

```
```

This is not an exhaustive list, so add other items as you go.

If you are fortunate enough to make it through to the assessment centre stage of the application process, then the best approach is to set out to enjoy the day! On the day the facilitators and assessors will do absolutely everything they can to make you feel at ease, and you can look forward to the chance to meet other candidates. Yes, it will be mentally challenging and tiring, but attend determined to give it your best shot; that way you will maximize your chances of success.

For obvious reason of cost these events feature late in the recruitment process, when the vast majority of candidates have been eliminated. You can take it that the Civil Service is very interested in you and they are prepared to invest a quite considerable sum of money in taking a long, careful look at your potential. They will seek to use the event to form as objective an assessment of you as they can. In their eyes you will no longer be another application form or test paper result but an individual whom they want to meet and get to know. They will also want you to be interested in them and to have thought carefully about why you want to join the Fast Stream. Unfortunately it is no long sufficient to tell a prospective employer that you have had a look at their website. Attend armed with the benefits of a careful, interested look at the organization overall, the section in which you would like to be placed and the position to which you have applied.

How the time you spend is organized and in what order you undertake the assessments will vary slightly between candidates because some will, for example, undertake the interview first, followed perhaps by the written exercise, while others will undertake the written assignment first and then the interview. Things are organized this way in order to manage resources efficiently and to reduce the time you spend hanging around waiting your turn. You will be informed of or directed to an outline of what your time will comprise. You can glean a lot of very useful information from this, especially from information about the competencies examined. Read between the lines and you will be able to plan your approach.

All the assessments will be competency based. What this means is that the assignment will be used to test a stated list of behaviour traits that are taken to be characteristic of a desired quality. These might include any number of features, including, for example, communication, drive, decision making, relationship building, team work and so on.

The relationships between the various assignments and the competencies can be set out in a matrix such as that shown in Table 7.1.

TABLE 7.1   Competency and assignment matrix

Competency tested	Determination	Development of ideas	Decision making	Planning	Teamwork	Written communication
1 Group exercise	*	*		*	*	*
2 Written exercise			*	*		*
3 Presentation		*	*			
4 Interview	*				*	

This serves to show the principle of the link between an assessment and the competencies it is used to investigate. In practice more competencies would be investigated than shown here.

Whatever you do, do not forget the most important thing to take with you when you attend the centre: suitable ID. For reasons of test security, administrators will want to be able to confirm that no one is impersonating you and attending on your behalf. Read and follow carefully the instructions on your invitation and contact the administrators if you have any questions. They will provide you with everything you need or are allowed in terms of pens, scrap paper, calculators and so on. It would be a big mistake to arrive late. So locate the centre and make sure you can find it with time to spare.

We will now consider in more detail and offer insight and tips as to how best to approach group exercises, presentations, written exercises and self-assessment exercises. You might also find the mock assessment centre at www.gradjobs.co.uk useful.

The group exercise or role play

The topic or topics you are assigned to discuss vary but otherwise you will find group exercises are fundamentally similar in that you will find yourself as one of a number of candidates and you must engage in consensual discussion.

Preparation time

Group exercises start with time to prepare. During the preparation time, list points that you feel are very important and make sure that these come up in the discussion. Don't worry if someone raises one of your points before you have the chance to do so; just contribute to its discussion and help develop the issue. Sometimes you will get to meet the other candidates before the exercise starts, and if you do, use this time to get to know them. You most likely will be told not to appoint a chairperson. Aim to play to your strengths: if maths is your thing, then use the data they give you to work out some relevant figures (though you should include figures even if maths is not your thing!). It is vital to listen to others. The assessors will be looking to see if your input helps to move the group forward, and whether you help the group to achieve its objectives.

In some cases you are given a great deal of briefing information – almost more than you can read in the time allowed. If this occurs, then review the material quickly and keep your notes very brief. You might decide on an assessment tool to help in the handling of the briefing papers. Examples include SWOT (strengths, weaknesses, opportunities, threats) and PEST (political, economic, social, technological) analyses. Another commonly used tool is the spider diagram, which is great for speed, recall and the emphasis of connections. Prepare these tools and think through these strategies before the day.

If you find that you do not have enough time to read all the background material, then decide what you want to say and use the time you have to make absolutely sure you have sufficient evidence to back it up. Don't forget to include figures.

You are likely to be briefed as a group, and this group will comprise the people with whom you will discuss the topics. If appropriate and the opportunity presents itself, take the trouble to get to know some of the group. This will really help with any nervousness you may suffer. You will find it so much easier to have a constructive conversation with someone you have talked with before.

The discussion

The discussion will be observed and notes taken by the assessors; it may even be recorded on video. Push all this out of your mind as much as possible and keep your thoughts on the group, its objective and the discussion.

Be careful and probably avoid taking notes yourself during the exercise. If you really must take notes, then keep them extremely brief – just one-word notes, as you really do not want the assessors to notice that you are looking down at them. You want them to observe lots of eye contact and nods in agreement on your part, and to conclude that you can listen and have understood the significance of the contribution of others by modifying your position to take account of their contribution.

If you can and the opportunity presents itself, then speak first so that you make the first impression and demonstrate drive. Don't worry if your position is entirely different from everyone else's – you are being assessed on how you make your case, not what case you are making. So set out to make as good a case as you can for the view that you are representing, but also point out its weaknesses. Make sure you are enthusiastic even when discussing what might seem very mundane issues.

Be assertive in getting your points across, but be very careful not to stray into language that could be taken as aggressive. Listen as well as talk. Do make lots of eye contact and do nod in agreement, but don't shake your head or demonstrate your disagreement through body language. Demonstrate that you can listen and have understood the significance of the contribution of others by modifying your position to take account of the contribution of others. Consider making explicit reference to how you have modified your case to take into account the contributions of others. Do this by, for example, offering supportive summaries of others' contributions, then adding a further relevant point of your own.

Recognize the talents and merit in other people's contributions without diminishing your own. Use 'us' and 'we' to emphasise collective purpose. Suggest criteria to clarify and evaluate the project. Help draw out quieter candidates by creating the space for them to speak. Do this by helping to ensure that everyone has a say and do show decisiveness and leadership qualities, but avoid adopting the role of chair.

Do not take criticism personally. Don't start or get sucked into an argument; but in the unlikely event that one occurs, do try to help make peace between the parties. This is important and a point on which many otherwise good candidates fail, so be sure to show empathy and go out of your way to resolve tension or disputes that arise between the other parties.

Be prepared to adopt the suggestions of others over your own, as this will be taken as an indication of your willingness to support another project, of flexibility and a talent in the building of relationships. Be constructive in your contributions and be supportive of others in your group. Keep your contributions to the point and spell out the relevance if you refer to something not immediately significant to the issue under discussion. Remember to back up all your points with facts and figures from the background material.

Self-evaluation of your performance

It is common for you to be asked to complete a self-assessment of your performance at an assessment centre. Take this exercise seriously, as it is often scored and counts towards your overall mark. If appropriate, comment on both what you learnt from it and on how you might improve, were you to attend the event or take the exercise again. Keep your self-criticism positive but be sure it is genuine. You might comment on, for example, how productive your relationship building was, what the impact of your communication was, or how the group might have better developed the assignment.

Many candidates find critical self-evaluation a challenge: we are all so used to hiding our weaknesses and promoting our strengths. But realize that otherwise very strong candidates do fail because they have not been open enough about their weaknesses and have not taken the opportunity to describe the strategies they have devised in order to address them.

Presentation

There is a lot you can do before the day to prepare for your presentation.

Plan something to say on core issues relevant to most subjects

There is a large number of core issues that are relevant to pretty well every scenario. They include, for example, recent legislation, the environment, health and safety, equality of opportunity, inclusiveness of people with disabilities (don't only think wheelchairs but include all types of disability) and social inclusion generally. There are bound to be cross-cutting themes relevant to the subject on which you are asked to present, so research them in advance. The opportunity may arise where you can refer to these issues and gain valuable points.

Decide in advance how you might structure your presentation

You will not know the subject of your presentation until perhaps a short time before you have to make it. But this does not mean that you cannot do some preparation around the possible structure you intend to use. In the introduction you may want to describe in summary what you intend to go on to say; then in your conclusion, review what you have said. There are some very good publications on the making of successful presentations that are worth a study.

You might decide to start by stating succinctly the assignment and go on to describe why addressing the issue is useful or necessary. If appropriate, you could then review the file material (people, budget, rules) or background. Headings after that point might include Actions, Recommendations, Alternatives, Conclusion. Do not forget that it is essential that you show enthusiasm throughout.

Practice at getting your timing right

You may not yet know how long you will have to present, but all the same it is worth practising how much you can say effectively in the usual time slots allocated in these exercises. On the day you will be allocated something between 10 and 20 minutes and you do not want to finish short or overrun. To get it right you need to have some experience of how long it will take to present a series of points with impact. Try to say too much or too little and you may end up disappointed with your presentation. Listen to a few public speakers on the radio, for example, and study how they make a point with impact and how long it takes them. You equally do not want to find yourself unable to cover all the points you planned to make and to be told to stop before you have made your concluding remarks.

Briefing and preparation time

You are provided with a briefing pack on the subject and time in which to prepare your presentation. Be warned that it is common for candidates to find the amount of time allowed for the study of the background papers to be very tight.

Be sure to present the difficulties as well as the advantages of your approach to the topic. Often you are asked to provide something original on the subject. Even if you are not specifically asked to do this, it may be worth offering a novel aspect to your presentation and then go on to examine the benefits and challenges to this aspect (don't forget to identify it as an original contribution). The relevance of everything you say should be clear or be explained. In practice, the assessors don't so much care what you decide on but judge you on how you explain, justify and criticize it.

Once you have decided what to say, then settle on your structure and make clear legible notes to which you can refer when making the presentation; and resolve to keep to this outline. Allocate an amount of time to each part of your presentation. Do not try to write out verbatim what you hope to cover. Even if you could manage it in the time allowed, the exercise is not about reading an essay aloud. Instead, try numbering your points and commit these numbers and the key words associated with them to memory. Try labelling them with one-word reminders and memorizing these. Try anything that works for you and will help you recall the points you want to make without excessive reference to your notes.

Remember to work quickly, as you may find you have very little time to prepare for your presentation.

Your presentation

Nerves aside, your presentation is likely to be as good or bad as your preparation both before the day and during the preparation time. The assessors are not expecting a polished public performance. But do be sure to speak clearly, make eye contact and try to keep reference to your notes to a minimum. Do think on your feet and adapt what you say as you speak, then revert back to your structure. Keep an eye on the time and try as much as possible to keep to the limits you set to speaking on each part of your presentation. If you find yourself going over time, then drop some points. As already said, it is important to deliver a timely presentation rather than be asked to stop before you reach your conclusions. You are very likely to get the opportunity to raise further points and add points of detail in the question-and-answer session that follows.

Follow-up questions and discussion

In these exercises it is common for more time to be spent answering questions and discussing with the assessor what you have said than you spent making your presentation.

It will help if you think of this time more as a brainstorming session than a cross-examination. So approach it with an open, curious mind rather than risk being perceived as defensive. During questions the assessors may follow up your response and keep asking follow-up questions until they feel they have the measure of you. At some point they will have decided you have made the grade but they may still keep asking questions until you run out of things to say. Don't let this undermine your self-confidence, and don't take offence. When the next line of questioning begins it's a fresh start, a new line of enquiry, and you should have a different line of responses. Avoid falling back on a previous response – ie avoid repeating yourself. At all times make sure your response is relevant to the question and the line of enquiry. Listening skills are as important here as they will be in the group exercise. Expect there to be one person who leads the questions and one or more others who mainly observe and take notes.

Self-assessment

If you are required to complete a self-assessment of your performance in the presentation exercise, then once again take it seriously and complete it to the best of your ability, as what you write may be scored and feature as part of your overall assessment. See the note on self-evaluation in the section on the group exercise or role play.

Written exercise

This is a test of your ability to handle information, organize it and communicate in writing. You will be presented with a file of papers that provide information on a subject. The paper may include conflicting information, which you have to evaluate and make recommendations about. Your task is to analyse the papers and prepare a note that builds a balanced and convincing case. To do this, you will need to compare and contrast the options, using the stated criteria or proposing your own, and explain convincingly the reasons for your recommendation. These exercises are nearly always completed on a computer, so make sure your keyboard skills are up to scratch.

Planning in advance

Again you can undertake some useful preparation before the day. One thing to consider is the style of approach that you adopt. This decision in part will depend on your background and your strengths. It is obvious that you should play to these. It should also take account of the type of Fast Stream position you would most like. For example, if you would prefer an economic or technology in business placement, then consider adopting a business style of report writing with an executive summary, stating the recommendation and summarizing the whole document, main body and then conclusion. If you would prefer a clerk's position in Parliament, then a university style of report may be more appropriate, with an elegant, fluid, readable written style. This way you will appear well suited to the position. If producing a written document is really not your thing, then consider using (but not excessively) bullet points and underlined headings to help convey your message. Illustrate points where applicable; they will then be far more convincing. If you find that you have not included numbers in your note, then you have probably not done as well as you could; wherever it is practical to do so, illustrate, back up and provide numerical evidence for what you say. The assessors will be looking for you to provide evidence of the case or point you make, so refer to figures or passages in the background paper and remember to give the source of references.

Before the day it may be useful to give thought to analytical tools or processes to which you might refer or that you might use in the exercise. SWOT and PEST analyses have already been mentioned. Consider if there are any core issues to which you might make reference in your paper that are applicable to most issues in the sector to which you are applying. Look at reports and studies on the internet to identify possible issues. These might include, for example, equality of opportunity, or how to reach the hard-to-reach or challenging members of our society, or the contributions and threats that technological advances might bring.

A common question is: 'How much should I write?' The answer is that, within reason, what actually matters is not how much you write but what you write. Don't write without good purpose and take care to use correct grammar, spellings and punctuation. Write too much and you increase the risk of errors and have less time to find any errors you might have made.

Briefing and preparation time

When you come to take the assignment you will be briefed on the exercise and provided with background or briefing papers. You may have a lot of information to go through and the time allowed to complete this part of the task may be tight. Be sure not to get caught out by the time limit, so clarify the aim of the exercise as explained to you; and, first and foremost, use the time to obtain the information necessary to serve the objective of the assignment. Then set about deciding the line to take in your paper and the structure that you will adopt.

The written assignment itself

Much of what you have done during your education and working career to date will serve you well in a written exercise. So take confidence from the fact that you have the skill to succeed in this assessment and apply what you have prepared before the day and during the briefing and preparation time. Although the written assignment is almost certainly to be administered on a PC, still think back to the written exams at school or university for an idea of what to expect and insight into the best approach. Start with a note of the structure that you have decided to adopt and then use your time to implement that plan. Take care over grammar and spelling. Remember, the assessors are looking to see how well you can structure an argument and examine a number of options, recommending one. Where appropriate, use illustrations to make your points, back up what you say with figures, and rather than quote from the background information, paraphrase it or restate the relevant passage in your own words. Demonstrate your ability at handling numerical information by offering clear, succinct restatements of relevant data in the background information. Remember to reference sources. Be convincing while remaining impartial and objective.

The interview

A typical Civil Service interview will involve a panel of two or sometimes three people asking you a set of structured questions. ('Structured' means that all candidates are asked the same basic questions but not necessarily the same follow-up questions.) Expect a typical competency-based interview; there will be no tricks or traps. You will pass or fail depending on how well you provide evidence of the competencies examined. You must recognize which competency each question relates to and provide an answer that convinces the interviewer that you have these competencies based on the evidence and examples you provide.

Your examples and evidence must tie in with what you have said on your application and you should not use the same example to illustrate more than one competency. Your examples can draw from any aspect of your past, eg work, study, home, hobbies. Provide detail to make your answer more convincing. For example, it is better to say, 'In March 2009 I was...' rather than, 'Recently I was...'

Relating to the sort of competencies examined, below are some example questions that you might face (they could obviously be different). The real questions may not be as difficult as the examples below, but in the real interview you may be suffering from some nervousness, so it is best to practice with something challenging:

Competency: results orientation:

- Can you tell us about an occasion when you had to achieve a set of goals within a set timescale?

Possible follow up questions:

- How were the goals measured?

- What would you have done if you had not realized all the goals?

- With the benefit of hindsight, how might you have approached the assignment differently in order to realize better results?

Competency: planning and prioritizing:

- Please tell us the key features of a plan that you would adopt in order to complete an assignment, and give us an example of when you have put such a plan into practice.

- Have you ever had to prioritize your work? If so, please tell us how you went about it.

Potential follow-up questions:

- What would you take into consideration if you had to change priorities?

- Can you give an example of when you had to revise your work to reprioritize its objectives? Tell us what you did and what the outcome was.

Competency: communicating and influencing:

- Can you describe to us a situation where you have influenced a decision-making process?

- Describe an instance when you have communicated how you felt to someone in a position of authority, how you went about it and the outcome.

- Can you tell us about an occasion when you have communicated your views to colleagues and how your contribution led to a positive result?

Competency: customer orientation:

- Why do you think a customer-orientated approach is important to our organization?

- Tell us about something you have done that involved putting the customer first. Be sure to tell us how this was achieved on a day-to-day basis.

CHAPTER 8

Answers and explanations

Answers and explanations for Chapter 2

Handling data: the essentials

1   East, all you need to answer this type of question is to know the points of the compass and the directions of clockwise and anticlockwise. Try drawing it out on a piece of paper if you did not get the right answer.

2   West

3   North

4   No, David could have made his turns in either direction in order to end up facing east.

5   75p, £3.00 divided by 4 = 75p.

6   28, £21 divided by £3 = 7 packs purchased. Multiply by 4 batteries per pack = 28 batteries.

7   £5.32, £1.33 multiplied by 4 = £5.32.

8   £18, £1.50 multiplied by 12 = £18.

9   16, 48 divided by 3 = 16.

10 £6.24, four boxes of eggs are needed. £1.56 multiplied by 4 = £6.24.

11 £5.20, the price of an egg is £1.56 divided by 6 = 26p. Multiply by 20 = £5.20.

12 360 g, 6 multiplied by 60 = 360.

13 200 g, weight of 1 egg is 300 g divided by 6 = 50 g. Multiply by 4 = 200 g.

14 11, £132 divided by 12 = 11.
15 40, divide 1,200 (p) by 30 (p) = 40.
16 £8.80, £16 multiplied by 0.55 = £8.80.
17 0.25 g, 400 divided by 1,600 = 0.25.
18 111 g, there are 37 × 10 = 370 beans. Multiply by the weight of each: 370 × 0.3 = 111 g.
19 £7.00, 25 multiplied by 28 = 700 pence or £7.00.
20 £66.66, 10.1p multiplied by 660 = 6,666 pence or £66.66.
21 £2.40, £48 × 5% = £2.40.
22 12, 100% = 60, 10% = 6; so 20% = 12.
23 80, 60 minutes divided by 3 = 20 buses per hour. Multiply by 4 = 80 per shift.
24 12 minutes, 6 hours consist of 360 minutes, which, divided by 30 = 12.
25 33.3%, 13 is a third of 39 or 33.3%.
26 7 minutes and 30 seconds, 45 multiplied by 10 = 450 seconds. Divided by 60 to convert to minutes = 7.5 or 7 minutes 30 seconds.
27 £22.50, £202.50 divided by 9 = £22.50.
28 £60, 4 multiplied by 30 = 120 divided by 2 = 60.
29 £13.44, £112 multiplied by 12 = £1,344, divided by 100 = £13.44.
30 Yes, the total VAT cost will be £2,100, which is 17.5% of £12,000.
31 27
32 Yes, 17.5% of 1,500,000 = 262,500.
33 1,125 ml
34 3.25 pm
35 30.6 euros
36 More, the vendor would receive about £326,000.
37 90, each litter of 9 multiplied by the 9 piglets = 81, to which you must add the original 9 piglets, giving you 90.
38 3%, a 1% increase is 5.3 schools, so an increase of 16 is equal to just over 3%.

Quantitative reasoning

1 C, multiply the price of one dozen by 3.5: 1.2 × 3.5 = 4.2.
2 D, to calculate the weight of a single parcel, divide the weight of two parcels by two: 0.5/2 = 0.25 kg. Take away the weight of a parcel from the combined weight of a parcel and a letter to get the weight of a letter: 0.35 − 0.25 = 0.1. Multiply by two for the weight of two letters: 0.1 × 2 = 0.2.
3 B, one-third of the full price is 33.33%. The remainder is 66.66%, so the discount was 66.66%.
4 F, one-quarter of £24,840 is £6,210. Add that quarter to the year 2000 profit: £24,840 + £6,210 = £31,050.

5   B, 64 − 25% = 48 and 16 − 25% = 12.

6   D, £277,000 − £67,000 − £21,000 − £103,000 = £86,000.

7   D, one coach can accommodate 75/3 = 25 passengers. Divide 150 by 25 = 6.

8   A, divide the total income by the number of people: £1,134/126 = £9.

9   D, Sophie spends 1 h 30 m travelling each way, equals 3 h every day. She works 5 days per week, so 3 × 5 = 15.

10   E, add up all the overtime hours: 2 + 1.5 + 1 + 2.5 + 3 = 10, then divide by the number of staff: 10/5 = 2.

11   D, £70 + 5% = £73.50 and £80 − 45% =£44. £73.50 + £44 = £117.50 per week.

12   F, multiply the number of coins by the fraction of a pound the coin represents: (7 × 1/2 = £3.50) + (18 × 1/5 = £3.60) + (33 × 1/10 = £3.30) + (12 × 1/20 = £0.60) + (15 × 1/50 = £0.30) = £11.30.

13   F, we can calculate the number of self-employed staff by finding out the percentage that 29 members of staff represent. The remaining 24% + 18% = 42%, therefore 29 = 58%. By dividing 29 by 58% we can find out 1%: 29/58 = 0.5 of a member of staff. By multiplying 24% by 0.5 we find out the number of self-employed staff = 12.

14   D, the ratio of investment between B and A is 1:2.5, therefore the total investment = 3.5. Divide £70,000 by 3.5 = £20,000 = 1 share = B's contribution.

15   C, divide the copies per machine per hour by 60 minutes: 180/60 = 3 copies per minute. One photocopier can produce 3 × 25 = 75 copies in 25 minutes. Two photocopiers can produce twice as much = 150 copies.

16   A, Angela spends 35 hours per week in the office (7 h × 5 days). Divide by 7 and multiply by 3: (35/7) × 3 = 15 hours per week typing letters.

17   C, 12 m × 18.5 m = 222 sq m × £2.25 = £499.50.

18   F, £64 as a percentage of £400 is 64/400 × 100 = 16%.

19   D, calculate the actual length in cm by multiplying 57.5 by 2,000 = 115,000 cm. To convert to metres, divide by 100: 115,000/100 = 1,150 m.

20   C, there are 3.5 times more female than male workers. 4 × 3.5 = 14.

21   D, the total amount needed for the trip is 400 euros × 4 days = 1,600 euros. To convert to sterling, divide by the exchange rate: 1,600/1.6 = £1,000.

22   A, John and Sarah together earn £46,700 (18,700 + 28,000). Mark earns 53% of this amount (47% less than John and Sarah). 1% = £467; 53% = £24,751.

23   B, 2000: £1,250 × 110% = £1,375. 2001: £1,375 × 110% = £1,512.50.

24   A, divide the total number of employees by the sum of the ratio: 370/10 = 37. Multiply by the 7 old: = 259.

25   C, the annual target is 150 sales × 4 quarters = 600. Average 137 per quarter × 3 quarters = 411. 600 − 411 = 189.

26   A, the £15,400 equals 100% minus 23% of the secretary's income = 77%. Her full income is 15,400/77 × 100 = £20,000.

27 E, first we need to find out how many people Company A employs. If Company C employs 25% fewer than A, then 120 = 75%; 120/75 = 1.6 × 100 = 160. Therefore Company A employs 160 people. Ratio A to B is 2:1, so Company B employs 160/2 = 80 people.

28 B, the office area is 11 m × 12.5 m = 137.5 sq m. Deduct the area underneath the cabinet: 125 cm × 80 cm = 10,000 sq cm, which converts to 1 sq m, so the area to be carpeted is 136.5 sq m. Four tiles 50 cm by 50 cm are required to carpet each sq m, so the total needed is 136.5 × 4 = 546.

29 E, £3,700 – 35% = £2,405. The amount of this proportion spent is 3/12 on the speaker and 8/12 on the transport = 11/12, so 1/12 is left for refreshments: 2,405/12 = £200.4167, which rounds to £200.

Data interpretation

1 D, can clearly be seen from table.
2 B, can clearly be seen from table.
3 D, 4.5 New Commonwealth + 3.1 rest of the world = 7.6 (thousand).
4 C, 3.9 (thousand) in 2000 – 3.7 (thousand) in 1985 = 0.2 (thousand) = 200.
5 B, 16/40 = 40%.
6 B, the ferry leaves Pier Head on the hour and returns 50 minutes later.
7 B, can clearly be seen from table.
8 E, between 3.50 pm and 4.15 pm.
9 D, 50 × £2.20 = £110.00.
10 E, a 15-minute delay on the last four journeys would result in an hour's delay overall, so the finish time is 6.15 pm + 1 hour = 7.15 pm.
11 D, can clearly be seen from table.
12 B, can easily be calculated from table.
13 D, 475 less 325.
14 C, 200°C × 105% = 210°C.
15 A, can clearly be seen from table: PURE ORANGE JUICEX1LTR.
16 D, 2 multisave items: £1.79 + £1.99 = £3.78.
17 E, although the total items indicated by 'g' add up to £8.27, there is a multisave of £1.79 on S SATSUMA LARGE; thus £8.27 – £1.79 = £6.48.
18 C, £302.60 × 10% = £30.26.
19 C, 23 days' entitlement – 1 taken last year – 11 taken in the current year = 11.
20 D, Hasan receives 26 days, which equal a basic 23 days for the first two years' service plus 3 more days. This is 1 day per year (half a day per half year) so he has been with the company for 3 plus 2 years = 5 years in total.
21 C, 23 days' annual entitlement – 1.5 days taken last year – 8 days taken in the current year = 13.5 days. £300/5 = £60 × 13.5 = £810.

22 E, S Brown has 23 less 12 days' holiday left (1 taken last year, 11 taken in the current year) = 11 days. If he takes these 11, he needs 4 more days of unpaid leave.

23 C, 31 (units sold) × £49 (price per package) = £1,519 sales income. 3% commission = £45.57.

24 A, 24 + 31 + 28 + 21 + 26 + 26 = 156/6 = 26.

25 E, the commission for the first 25 units is calculated at 3% and equals £36.75. The commission for the three units achieved over the target is calculated at 5% and equals £7.35. This gives a total of £44.10.

26 E, four out of 6 employees reached the target.

27 C, the most profitable product is identified by subtracting the total cost from the sales price.

28 D, reducing the manufacturing cost of £2 by 50% will add £1 to the sales revenue for each unit sold. So the sales revenue is the existing £37,625 plus £21,500 = £59,125.

29 B, £7.99 – £5.37 = £2.62 (revenue per unit) × 11,750 (number of units) = £30,785.

30 A, 23% of £743,578.00 = £171,022.94 tax paid. £743,578.00 – £171,022.94 = £572,555.06 net profit.

31 A, (0 + 10 + 21.5 + 4)/4 = 8.9 approx.

32 B, 3.5 – (–1) = 4.5°C.

33 C

34 F, Cumulative temperature in 2000: (1.5 + 15.5 + 23 + 2) = 42. Final quarter 2001 is 42 – 2 – 14.5 – 25 = 0.5.

Word swap

1	movement/tone		**11**	eat/respect
2	work/result		**12**	kill/catch
3	artificial/natural		**13**	rake/forget
4	some/and		**14**	numerous/bitter
5	remain/recess		**15**	adaptable/Roman
6	most/each		**16**	inserted/impervious
7	to/is		**17**	idyllic/irritating
8	style/hunger		**18**	known/health
9	over/now		**19**	about/without
10	by/of			

Missing words

1	B, effect effect	**12**	D, piece pierce
2	C, dependent dependant	**13**	B, inform infirm
3	B, accepted licence	**14**	B, practice practise
4	B, conscience conscious	**15**	A, stationary stationery
5	A, threw rear	**16**	D, receipt recipe
6	B, hew hue	**17**	D, exercises immediately
7	C, principle principal	**18**	B, minor operate
8	A, courtesy curtsy	**19**	A, boys boys'
9	B, dispensary disciplinary	**20**	B, it's its
10	C, hoard horde	**21**	B, plumb straight
11	C, flowers flour		

Correct sentences

1   A. If you're looking for an evening out this month, there are big offers on musicals and pop concerts.

2   B. The consumer is protected from exploitation by a given seller by the existence of other sellers from whom he can buy.

3   C. All mammals produce eggs within which their young develop.

4   A. There are maps and travel books available for most of England's towns and cities.

5   C. Further information will be given to you when you visit the head office.

6   A. She married again, which surprised everybody who knew her.

7   B. There is a wide selection of gifts available, all of which can be ordered by post or online.

8   A. At that moment, I wished I had gone to the same university as John.

9   C. When I go to university I will have no time for reading novels.

10   B. The coach was expecting great things of the team this season.

11   A. Whenever a new book comes out she is the first to buy a copy.

12   B. There is the promise of a more secure future for those who save on a regular basis.

13   C. If the customer should return the goods, you must ensure you check them before giving a refund.

14   B. There are places where that kind of behaviour is unacceptable.

15   A. This borough is very good about providing bins for recycling metal, plastic, glass and paper.

16   C. One of the most important notes on the piano is Middle C.

17   B. Once Simon gets angry it takes a long while for him to calm down.

18   A. We pitched our tent on the bank of the river Stour, near where it joins the Avon.

19   C. They were walking along the beach all day yesterday and they will be walking along the cliff all day tomorrow.

20   A. It was Galileo who discovered that Jupiter has moons.

Following procedures

1	B		**6**	D
2	E		**7**	G, H
3	E		**8**	F
4	D		**9**	E, F, I
5	E, G, H		**10**	D

Speed and accuracy

1	B, 3 pairs		**13**	B, 3 pairs
2	E, none		**14**	A, all 4
3	C, 2 pairs		**15**	A, all 4
4	E, none		**16**	A, all 4
5	C, 2 pairs		**17**	B, 3 pairs
6	E, none		**18**	B, 3 pairs
7	C, 2 pairs		**19**	C, 2 pairs
8	D, 1 pair		**20**	C, 2 pairs
9	B, 3 pairs		**21**	D, 1 pair
10	C, 2 pairs		**22**	D, 1 pair
11	E, none		**23**	D, 1 pair
12	C, 2 pairs			

Answers and explanations for Chapter 3

Practice test 1: quantitative reasoning

1   F, $(7 \times 27) + (4 \times 19) = 265p = £2.65$.

2   D, $14.45 + 27 m = 15.12$.

3   F, end of year 1: $1,000.00 \times 105\% = £1,050.00$. End of year 2: $1,050.00 \times 105\% = £1,102.50$. End of year 3: $1,102.50 \times 105\% = £1,157.63$.

4   C, end of year 1: $800 - 40\% = £480$. End of year 2: $480 - 25\% = £360$. End of year 3: $360 - 25\% = £270$.

5   F, 30 wpm $\times$ 30 minutes $= 900$ words.

6   E, 1.25 × 4 = 5.

7   D, (2 × 1.75) + (5 × 1.15) = 9.25 × 1.175 = £10.87.

8   B, 18,900/9 = 2,100. 2,100 × 3 = 6,300.

9   D, 1 kg/5 = 200 g. £3.50/5 = £0.70.

10 A, the return journey takes 1.5 hours. The meeting takes another 1.5 hours. The total time spent away from the office is 3 hours.

11 D, 20% = 1 in 5, so 10 members of staff must join to qualify for two free memberships.

12 C, the price of two items = 100%. If one item is free, 50% is saved.

13 C, 3.4/4.3 = 0.79 × 2.3 = £1.82.

14 B, the question requires you to find the time difference between 38/47 of an hour and 29/38 of an hour. These fractions can be treated as convenient equivalents to 4/5 and 3/4 of an hour = 48 and 45 minutes. Hence, 3 minutes' difference.

15 F, if £24 is 3%, then 1% is 24/3 = £8, and 100% = £800.

16 D, the new price is £10 − 25% = £7.50. £1,000/£7.50 = 133.33. The sales should increase by 33.3%.

17 E, the ratio of staple boxes can be expressed as 1:1.5:2.25:3.375, which sums to 8.125. 1,000 g/8.13 = 123 × 3.375 = 415.125 g.

18 C, 3.5% of 1,000 = £35. To obtain £35 commission, B must sell 35/.03 goods, which is £116.67 worth.

19 E, the time difference between Dubai and New York is 10 hours. It is 10 hours earlier in Dubai, so the conference will start at 04.30 am on 11 January.

20 F, the ratio is 2:7:1 which can also be expressed as 1:3.5:0.5.

21 D, 100/20 = 5 × 3 = 15%.

22 F, 7.99 × 0.305 = £2.44.

23 B, 225/0.45 = 500.

24 C, in 30 minutes it will travel 17.5 miles, which divided by 0.621 equals 28 km approximately.

25 C, £12/25 = £0.48 per minute. £0.48 × 45 = £21.60.

26 E, if 1 ft = 0.305 m, then 1 sq ft = (0.305 × 0.305) sq m = 0.093 sq m. Price per sq m: £6.25/0.093 = £67.20. Price for 5 sq m = £67.20 × 5 = £336.

27 D, {35 mph + (35/2)}/2 = 52.5/2 = 26.25.

28 B, (5,000 + 1,000) × 2 = 12,000. (12,000 + 1,000) × 2 = £26,000.

29 F, 1.83 m = (1.83/0.305) = 6 ft. 12 files per ft, so 6 × 12 = 72 files can be stored.

30 B, distance/time 56 miles/70 minutes = 0.8 miles per minute. 0.8 miles per minute × 60 minutes = 48 mph.

Practice test 2: data interpretation

1   B, readily seen from table.

2   D, 64 + 39 + 95 + 40 + 17 + 14 = 269.

3   D, 33/200 × 100 = 16.5%.

4   C, 42/300 × 100 = 14%, the lowest percentage.

5   E, 280 rand/selling price 3.18 = £88.05.

6   B, 1,750.00 × 2.99 – 4.5% = 4,997.03.

7   E, 4,997.03/2.79 = 1,791.05 – 4.5% = 1,710.45.

8   A, (1.55 +1.66)/2 = 1.605 average rate. 0.5 euros/1.605 = £0.31.

9   D, 1/6 = 16.66%.

10   F, £1 per week × 26.5 = £26.50.

11   C, £23.45 – £20 + £800 – £95 = £708.45.

12   A, – £250 + £360 – £25 = £85.

13   C, A package to Aberdeen = £1.66 + £0.85 = £2.51. A letter to France = £0.37.

14   A, 0.96 kg = 960 g = 500 g + 460 g. 500 (£1.66) + 250 (£0.85) + 210 (£0.85) = £3.36.

15   F, 100 g to Europe = £0.99 + 350 g to UK = £1.30 = £2.29.

16   E, Separately: £1.05 + £1.79 = £2.84. Together: £2.16 + £1.25 = £3.41. Difference: £0.57.

17   B, If there were 9.2 deaths per 1,000, then there were 9,200 deaths per million. Since there are 83 million people in Germany = 9,200 × 83 = 763,600.

18   B, Total births – total deaths = 3 per thousand = 3,000 deaths per million = 3,000 × 60 = 180,000.

19   C, End of 2001 = 60,180,000 total population. End of 2002 = 60,180,000 × 100. 3% = 60,360,540.

20   E, total births – total deaths per year.

21   F, arable land, permanent pasture and woodland = 33%. Therefore 67% of land = 545,630 × 67% = 365,572 sq km.

22   C, 1 km = 0.625 miles. 1 sq km = 0.39 sq m. 41,526 × 0.39 = 16,195.14.

23   F, 7,643/41,526 = 18.4%.

24   F, 30% of 504,782.

Practice test 3: correct sentences

1   B. If she had only listened to me, this would never have happened.

2   C. There are just three things you need to know about Jack.

3   B. If I were you I'd see a doctor.

4   A. It looks like everyone has gone to the cinema.

5   B. Either Jane or her sister is bringing the dessert.

6   C. If I hadn't had my seatbelt on I would be dead.

7   B. From Thursday you cannot have either the blue or the black pens.

8   A. I have been informed that neither Mandy nor Helen will be able to be there on Saturday.

9   B. Owning a dog is very different from owning a cat.

10   D. None of these.

11   C. If you were to go fishing at night you might find that you caught more fish than during the day.

12   A. Although the house and barn are on the same property, they will be sold separately.

13   D. None of these.

14   B. The managing director wanted you and me to attend the meeting.

15   B. Each night before I go to bed I make myself a cup of cocoa.

16   A. Carol thought it an honour to receive an MBE.

17   C. It looks as if it is going to rain.

18   B. Every one of the new computers in the main office has been virus checked.

19   C. It is equally as important to check your credit card statement as it is your bank statement.

20   C. Mike always seems to do it that way.

Practice test 4: following procedures

Situation 1

1   E (Mr D Fryer), the rules state that only the regional director can approve purchases from a non-approved supplier, and this supplier is not on the approved list.

2   B (Tom Mosby), area managers can approve purchases for their area only from approved suppliers to a maximum of £100,000.

3   A and B (Diana Jordan and Alex Matthews), administrative officers can approve expenditure in their area with approved suppliers to a maximum of £1,000.

4   E, only Maria Key is not allowed to approve this purchase.

5   B, the rules state that any expenditure over £100,000 must be approved by the appropriate area manager and the regional director.

Situation 2

6   D, the terms state that a 20% fee is charged up to £19,999 and 25% on salaries over £20,000. But the percentage charged on salaries of £20,000 is not given.

7   B, it is stated in the terms that a 50% rebate applies if the employee leaves after eight weeks but before 12 weeks of employment.

8   F, you can calculate the apportioned pro-rata amount due as 50% of the annual salary = $16,000 \div 2 = £8,000$ plus the £2,000 for the benefit of the car, and the 15% tax.

Situation 3

9   C and E, the procedures state that a final reminder is issued on the 15th work-ing day and that an invoice becomes overdue at that point. In the text prior to the procedures, it is stated that at the weekly meeting with Mr Jones accounts with overdue invoices should be reviewed.

10   B and D, it is stated in the situation that Mrs Smith and her assistant Tina hold this responsibility.

11   D, the passage states that the pair decide whether or not to refer an account to the company's firm of solicitors for advice as to whether there is a case for issuing legal proceedings. This is not the same as the options given in the suggested answers.

Situation 4

12   C, note that the questions ask which of the suggested answers would *least* support the applicant's case. C would least support the case because rule 5 makes it clear that under these circumstances the tribunal would find the case to have failed.

13   A, in these circumstances you would expect the tribunal to apply rule 4 and ask the employer to explain the unequal treatment.

14   B, assuming that the tribunal accepted the employer's explanation, then according to rule 4 the application would fail despite the fact that there was evidence of different treatment.

Situation 5

15   C, this is stated in rule 4.

16   C, while the maximum charge shown is 1.25%, this does not mean that there is a rule capping any charge above this amount.

17   B, he has been undercharged, not overcharged; the fee should have been charged at 1/365th of 1.25% of his fund.

Practice test 5: speed and accuracy

1	B, 2 pairs		**9**	E, none
2	C, 3 pairs		**10**	E, none
3	C, 3 pairs		**11**	C, 3 pairs
4	E, none		**12**	E, none
5	A, 1 pair		**13**	A, 1 pair
6	D, 4 pairs		**14**	B, 2 pairs
7	C, 3 pairs		**15**	A, 1 pair
8	A, 1 pair		**16**	D, 4 pairs

17	B, 2 pairs	
18	A, 1 pair	
19	E, none	
20	C, 3 pairs	
21	E, none	
22	A, 1 pair	
23	D, 4 pairs	
24	A, 1 pair	
25	D, 4 pairs	
26	A, 1 pair	
27	B, 2 pairs	
28	A, 1 pair	
29	E, none	
30	A, 1 pair	
31	B, 2 pairs	
32	D, 4 pairs	
33	B, 2 pairs	

34 A, 1 pair
35 B, 2 pairs
36 A, 1 pair
37 A, 1 pair
38 D, 4 pairs
39 E, none
40 E, none
41 C, 3 pairs
42 B, 2 pairs
43 D, 4 pairs
44 D, 4 pairs
45 E, none
46 E, none
47 A, 1 pair
48 C, 3 pairs
49 B, 2 pairs
50 E, none

Answers and explanations for Chapter 4

Situational awareness tests

Situation 1

1	2	3	4
C	B	B	C

Explanation: response 1 is less than acceptable because it will mean that the individual is left unaccompanied in the building. Responses 2 and 3 are acceptable responses (neither can be identified as the most appropriate response), as any potential breach in security will be addressed . Response 4 is less than acceptable because it will mean that a potential breach of security has been ignored.

Situation 2

1	2	3	4
C	C	C	A

Explanation: response 1 is less than acceptable because it involves your disclosing personal details of your staff to a colleague. Response 2 is less than acceptable because a team meeting is not a suitable event in which to discuss with an individual an issue such as body odour. Response 3 is less than acceptable because the fact that someone else has also noticed the odour means that you can no longer ignore the situation. Response 4 is the best because it will address the issue in a confidential and appropriate manner.

Situation 3

1	2	3	4
C	A	B	C

Explanation: response 1 is less than acceptable because a threat of violence is a serious matter and should not be ignored. Response 2 is the most appropriate because it will guarantee that the matter is dealt according to the correct procedure. Response 3 is an acceptable response because it will ensure that the matter is acted on. Response 4 is less than acceptable because it would be unreasonable to expect the person who was threatened to have to resolve the matter themselves and without the support of management.

Situation 4

1	2	3	4
B	B	A	C

Explanation: response 1 shows an ability to offer a compelling argument, which is a valued quality in a Fast Streamer and would be an acceptable first step. Response 2 would also be an acceptable initial response because it would draw on the experience of the steering group. Response 3 is the most appropriate response as it would demonstrate negotiation skills that are prized in a Fast Streamer and would most likely gain the commitment of the steering group to try again to make a success of the project as well as secure the required resources needed to deliver a successful project. Response 4 would be less than acceptable as it would only address the issue of incompatible data rather than the more pressing issue of the continuation of the project.

Situation 5

1	2	3	4
B	C	C	A

Explanation: response 1 is acceptable but may risk inflaming the situation, so is therefore not necessarily the most appropriate response. Responses 2 and 3 are both less than acceptable because they do not prevent the person from using further bad language.

Situation 6

1	2	3	4
C	C	B	A

Explanation: responses 1 and 2 are less than acceptable because they do not involve team working and the devising of strategy collaboratively. Responses 3 and 4 ensure the input of the whole team and so are likely to produce strategies that the team better understand and can work. Response 4 is the most appropriate because it places the most emphasis on working collaboratively.

Situation 7

1	2	3	4
C	C	A	C

Explanation: responses 1, 2 and 4 only offer the re-communication of the assigned roles and do not allow for the possibility that the assignment of roles could be improved or that duplication or conflict of roles since the reorganization may be the cause of the tension between the two workers. Response 3 is the most appropriate because it seeks the views of the individuals concerned as well as reviewing the assignment of roles.

Situation 8

1	2	3	4
A	C	C	C

Explanation: theft is a serious matter and response 1 is the most appropriate given that a theft has occurred. Responses 2 and 4 are less than acceptable because they do not attribute sufficient importance to the situation, and response 3 is less than acceptable because you may well not have the authority to search another member of staff's personal belongings or pockets. It would be better to leave this to the police.

Situation 9

1	2	3	4
C	A	C	B

Explanation: response 1 is less than acceptable because it fails to show diligence in the face of a setback. Response 2 is the most appropriate because it involves the team in deciding if there are the time and resources to reissue the contracts. Response 3 is less than acceptable because it lacks shared responsibility for putting the set-back right. Response 4 is acceptable but not the best response because while it shows leadership and diligence, it lacks a team approach.

Situation 10

1	2	3	4
C	C	C	A

Explanation: if the reorganization is to go well, then clear directions must be given, so for this reason response 4 is the most acceptable. Only response 4 would ensure that the reorganization was well managed and so the other responses are less than acceptable.

Situation 11

1	2	3	4
C	C	A	C

Explanation: response 1 would be less than acceptable because it would involve disclosing the personal circumstances of the individual to the team. Response 2 would be less than acceptable because you would first have to see if you could arrange things differently before you agreed to the request. Response 4 is less than acceptable because treating everyone equally does not mean that you cannot accommodate differences or people's changing circumstances.

Situation 12

1	2	3	4
B	B	C	C

Explanation: responses 1 and 2 are both acceptable because they maintain the confidentiality of the other project while making it clear that you do not agree that the failure of the wind farm proposal would mean that the land would be used for an offenders' institute. Response 3 would be less than acceptable because it might leave the impression that what the other speaker said was correct. Response 4 would be less than acceptable because it would be untrue.

Situation 13

1	2	3	4
A	B	B	C

Explanation: the Civil Service most values practical solutions that have been devised collaboratively. Responses 2 and 3 are collaborative in that they involve a sub-group of people but they are less appropriate than a response that involves the whole team. Response 4 is less than appropriate because it lacks collaboration.

Situation 14

1	2	3	4
B	C	A	C

Explanation: response 1 is acceptable because it clarifies the worker's role and responsibilities and invites him to come and talk some more. Responses 2 and 3 are less than acceptable because they do not offer the worker the support and help a manager should offer a worker. Response 3 is the most appropriate because it invites his view on what might help and offers to reorganize things differently.

Situation 15

1	2	3	4
A	C	C	C

Explanation: response 1 is the most appropriate because it offers to organize things in a way that best accommodates our differences and in this instance disabilities. Response 2 is less than appropriate because equality of opportunity does not mean that we do not make exceptions or arrange things differently to accommodate differences between us. Responses 3 and 4 are also less than acceptable because both present the disability as a problem and a matter of concern.

Situation 16

1	2	3	4
C	B	A	C

Explanation: discrimination against an applicant on the basis of gender is a matter that would need to be undertaken with great care to ensure that it was fair (in the vast majority of situations it would not be fair). Responses 1 and 4 therefore are less than acceptable because they do not seek clarification or advice on such a serious matter. Response 3 is the most acceptable because it involves the advice of a specialist. Response 2 is acceptable because it involves referring to the written documents and procedure for guidance before making the decision.

Situation 17

1	2	3	4
C	C	A	B

Explanation: a mastery of numerical data is highly valued in the Civil Service but the analysis of the pilot projects or the proposal of performance indicators would be less than acceptable as one of the first things you do in relation to your work on this new project. Response 3 would be the most appropriate as good team working would be essential for the future success of the project. The development of a programme of work and time frame would also be an acceptable first objective.

Situation 18

1	2	3	4
C	B	B	C

Explanation: response 1, to remove the school's records from the database, would be a less than appropriate response because it would not seek to establish the extent of the problem or bring a project-wide solution to it. Responses 2 and 3 are acceptable because they seek either to address the problem across the project or to establish its extent. Response 4 is less than acceptable because the educational aims of the project are not being well served if the children are taking inaccurate readings.

Situation 19

1	2	3	4
C	A	C	B

Explanation: response 1 is less than acceptable because someone might slip on the stairs before maintenance has a chance to repair them. Response 2 is the best response because the signs might prevent an accident in the meanwhile. Response 2 is less than acceptable because it is likely that you do not have the authority to instruct your staff to all work from home. This is something you would have first to agree with senior management. Response 4 is acceptable but not the most acceptable because staff are likely to use the stairs before they have read your e-mail.

Situation 20

1	2	3	4
B	C	A	C

Explanation: response 1 is acceptable because it includes in the review the whole team but it is not the most acceptable because it does not include representatives from other organizations (see response 3). Response 2 would be less than acceptable because it lacks a collaborative approach, and response 4 would be less than acceptable because it does not seek to learn form the setback of the first set of results.

Situation 21

1	2	3	4
A	C	C	C

Explanation: response 2 would be less than appropriate because if the advice is taken the offenders are denied the chance of gaining employment even if that chance is a remote one. Responses 3 and 4 are less than acceptable because they involve the suggestion that the offenders do not disclose their offences or only disclose them if asked, and such a suggestion lacks integrity. Response 1 is the most appropriate because it simply presents the facts.

Situation 22

1	2	3	4
C	B	C	A

Explanation: responses 1 and 3 would be less than acceptable because neither relies on any sort of investigation. Response 2 is acceptable because it takes the complaint seriously and involves an investigation. Response 4 is the most acceptable because it involves the most complete investigation.

Situation 23

1	2	3	4
C	B	C	A

Explanation: responses 1 and 3 would be less than acceptable because most line managers would want to be informed immediately of a development that had serious implications for a project. Response 2 would be acceptable because it would treat the development with suitable urgency while informing the line manager of the developments. Response 4 would be most acceptable because it would allow the manager to agree the urgent action.

Situation 24

1	2	3	4
A	C	C	B

Explanation: most organizations have clear procedures for dealing with the press. Dealing with the journalist's request without referring to the organization's public relations procedure risks exceeding your authority, making responses 2 and 3 less than acceptable. Response 1 is the best response because as well as finding out the correct procedure it obtains the telephone number of the journalist, which means their identity can be confirmed. Response 4 would be acceptable because it will result in the correct procedure being followed.

Situation 25

1	2	3	4
C	A	B	C

Explanation: response 1 is less than acceptable because by checking their own files they are unlikely to find their own omissions or mistakes. Response 2 is the best response because it involves taking ownership of the state of the records and is the response most likely to identify errors or omissions prior to the full audit. Response 3 is acceptable because it may well succeed in the identification of errors and omissions. Response 4 is less than acceptable because it risks demonstrating a lack of diligence.

Situation 26

1	2	3	4
A	B	C	C

Explanation: response 1 is the most appropriate because it prioritizes team building and will ensure that the team and you get to know each other. Response 2 is acceptable but places less emphasis on team building. Responses 3 and 4 are less than acceptable because they place no emphasis on the need to build the new team.

Situation 27

1	2	3	4
C	A	C	C

Explanation: If you are discontented in your role, then you should draw this to the attention of your line manager as soon as is practical so that they have the chance to correct the situation. You should not wait until an annual review to do this or ignore how you feel while getting on with the job.

Situation 28

1	2	3	4
C	B	B	B

Explanation: to send confidential papers to a newspaper would be a serious breach of confidentiality on your part and may well result in disciplinary or even criminal action against you. Any of the other responses would be acceptable and would help resole the matter positively.

Situation 29

1	2	3	4
C	C	B	A

Explanation: response 1 would be less than acceptable because the team would expect you to provide full disclosure of the facts. Response 2 would amount to fraud. Response 3 would be acceptable but is not the most acceptable response because it does not take the opportunity to try and correct the problem. Response 4 is the most acceptable because it is proactive and seeks to ensure that the supplier complies with the terms of the funding.

Situation 30

1	2	3	4
C	C	B	A

Explanation: responses 1 and 2 almost certainly mean that you would exceed your authority and allow a precedent to become established, which the human resource department would not welcome. Response 3 is acceptable but given the history of the case is unlikely to result in a lasting improvement in timekeeping. Response 4 is the most acceptable as it seeks advice from a specialist. The consequences of that meeting are not something that you should concern yourself with.

Personality questionnaires

1   *Explanation*: if this is true of how you act in work, then you must agree with the statement even though impulsiveness is not a sought-after quality of civil servants. If, like most people, you have done things you afterwards regret and might be impulsive on occasions at home with family or friends but not at work, then be sure to disagree.

2   *Explanation*: either emotional or insensitive are positive qualities in a civil servant; however, as someone applying for a senior managerial position, it would be better to be considered emotional rather than insensitive when it comes to the feelings of others. If you can do so, then it would be better to agree with this statement.

3   *Explanation*: to agree with this statement might, along with other responses, be used to conclude that you are reluctant to experiment or try new things in general. To agree with this statement on its own would not undermine your application; however, a series of responses along the same lines may suggest that you prefer the known and would find change difficult, and such a trait would not support your application.

4   *Explanation*: to be thin-skinned is to be easily upset and there is a risk that someone thin-skinned may find the pressure and daily experience of a managerial position in the Civil Service hard to deal with.

5   *Explanation*: civil servants work collaboratively and this suits the naturally gregarious. For this reason, to disagree with this statement is likely to be the preferred response.

6   *Explanation*: this statement is about a single heartfelt voice that goes against the majority view. To disagree with the statement would suggest you were principled and had integrity, and such qualities are highly regarded in the Civil Service.

7   *Explanation*: to agree with this statement may suggest that you are reserved and unapproachable, and these are qualities that would not support an application to a managerial position in the Civil Service.

8   *Explanation*: to be practical is to be sensible and have a realistic approach. To disagree with this statement allows you to be both practical and compassionate, while to agree suggests that you are more practical than compassionate. Both attributes would be valued in the service.

9   *Explanation*: tactful means diplomatic, considered and careful, and these personal qualities are highly rated in the Civil Service.

10 *Explanation*: this common saying means it does not matter how something is achieved; all that really matters is that it is achieved. Such a stance risks the conclusion that you lack principles and such a conclusion would not enhance your application.

11 *Explanation*: the views of someone qualified in a subject may carry more weight than the views of someone unqualified, but this should not lead you to agree with the statement that only those qualified should contribute to a debate.

12 *Explanation*: to leave a situation when events are changing fast may well amount to leaving when your contribution is most needed. Someone in a managerial position in the Civil Service would be expected to bring their experience and expertise to the challenge and not leave it to others.

13 *Explanation*: agreement with this statement does not imply that you lack patience because we all sometimes feel frustrated with others, and in fact it is a credit to you if, while you admit to sometimes feeling frustrated, when you do so you regret it.

14 *Explanation*: Your colleagues and managers will want to know all the facts and to hold back information on the basis that you believe someone will not want to hear something is likely to give rise to problems.

15 *Explanation*: you should disagree with this statement if you are primarily motivated in your career to earn a large salary. In the Civil Service the overall package can be good but this is not the first and foremost consideration of most civil servants.

16 *Explanation*: to be courteous is to be considerate and polite, and even in an emergency we should maintain these qualities.

17 *Explanation*: senior managers do carry a disproportionate share of responsibility but every member of a team should feel a shared sense of responsibility, and to agree with this statement risks the impression that you might be reluctant to take your share of responsibility. Such an impression would not support an application for a managerial position.

18 *Explanation*: Everyone makes mistakes, but to admit that we allow ourselves to be so distracted that we make them would not support an application for a managerial position in the service.

19 *Explanation*: both teamwork and keeping abreast of policy developments are important to the role of a manager in the Civil Service. Therefore, by not agreeing with the statement you can avoid the trap of having to rank one above the other.

20 *Explanation*: it is quite possible that the views of a new member of staff are equal to or more important than those of someone with long service. For example, the newcomer might be a specialist member of staff, such as a lawyer or accountant, providing technical advice. On the basis of the information provided, therefore, it is not appropriate to agree with the statement.

21   *Explanation*: you should readily disagree with this statement. Managers should be used to priorities changing and having to interrupt what they are doing to do something else.

22   *Explanation*: if this is a quality you possess, then have the confidence to disclose it, because a careful, considered approach is valued in the Civil Service.

23   *Explanation*: in the Civil Service being able to deal with people in a delicate and diplomatic fashion is considered more desirable than a bold and decisive style of working.

24   *Explanation*: civil servants often deal with complex matters that demand a compromise of one sort or another. A civil servant who is reluctant to make a compromise might well find it difficult to work collaboratively and reach a consensus.

25   *Explanation*: 'matter of fact' means straightforward, while 'down to earth' means unpretentious. Both are positive attributes that would be valued in a manager in the Civil Service. The choice between the two qualities is difficult but 'down to earth' might be preferable, as 'matter of fact' can imply a lack of compassion.

26   *Explanation*: to agree with this statement suggests that you cannot accept at face value what people say and that you must establish their motive before you can realize what they truly mean. Such a view implies an untrusting, suspicious approach.

27   *Explanation*: most roles, including managerial ones, involve a degree of repetition and to disagree with this statement risks the impression that you might struggle in many roles in the Civil Service.

28   *Explanation*: to say one thing and do another would never be regarded as acceptable in the Civil Service, as it would imply insincerity.

29   *Explanation*: to be wary is to be suspicious and distrustful, while someone who is naïve is inexperienced or youthful. Neither quality is desirable in a managerial role, but on balance being naïve might be forgivable, while to be wary might mean the person finds it hard to show the required understanding to manage others well.

30   *Explanation*: to be approachable is to be easy to talk to, which is a good quality in a manager. To be polite is also a desirable quality and means that you are respectful. But on balance, perhaps approachable is the more desirable of the two qualities.

Attitudinal tests

1   *Explanation*: if you admit that you could not follow every aspect of the Civil Service's equal-opportunities policy, then expect your application to be rejected.

2   *Explanation*: you should disagree with this statement if there are other reasons why you do not steal. You might, for example, believe that it is wrong.

3   *Explanation*: to disagree with this statement implies an ageist attitude. People adjust to change in different ways and at different rates and these differences are not linked to the age of the individual concerned. It is not true, for example, that only older workers find change hard or that the workers who find change the most difficult to adjust to are also the oldest workers.

4   *Explanation*: imagine yourself living in a community that speaks a language you cannot speak. If you were trying to deal with a civil servant, then you would want that individual to assist you as much as possible and to uphold the principle that they will provide you with the same duty of care and service despite the language barrier.

5   *Explanation*: bad language in work is never acceptable, no matter the circumstances, and you must help your staff find other more appropriate ways to deal with a stressful day.

6   *Explanation*: this is a question of honesty and a very high standard of honesty is expected of civil servants. For this reason you might well be expected to disagree with this statement.

7   *Explanation*: to show disdain is to show contempt and no matter the provocation this would not be an appropriate response from a civil servant in a higher managerial position.

8   *Explanation*: to show a client disrespect is inappropriate and the fact that the client is extremely challenging does not change this. You should not be tempted to make an exception; your staff must treat all clients with the same high professional standard.

9   *Explanation*: it is true that we all make mistakes; however, most managers want to hear about the problem straight away and not at some later point in time.

10   *Explanation*: it would be best to disagree with this statement as it would be better if you informed the person who asked you to undertake the new task that you were already very busy. You should also establish from the person if the new task could wait until you had completed you current work or if the new task should take priority over your current work.

11   *Explanation*: a racist remark is never appropriate.

12   *Explanation*: jokes and humour have a value in the workplace as they can, for example, help build a team. However, jokes about someone's sexuality would not be appropriate and as a manager you would be expected to discourage such comments.

13   *Explanation*: a lot of people may not think that taking pens and paper from work is stealing, but it is, and no employer would want a manager to allow such actions.

14   *Explanation*: to say that your actions speak louder than your words is to suggest that your word is not as reliable as your actions, and this is not a quality that the Civil Service looks for in a manager.

15 *Explanation*: any form of racism is unacceptable and pretending that you did not hear the joke would not be an appropriate response from someone in a managerial position.

16 *Explanation*: to a great extent civil servants work according to procedures and the service looks for employees who work well under such a culture.

17 *Explanation*: the presence of a woman in the team, attractive or otherwise, should have no bearing on how men in the team act. If they do try to impress her it could amount to harassment and might result in disciplinary action.

18 *Explanation*: derisory means nasty and it would be wrong and not clever to say something nasty.

19 *Explanation*: the Civil Service expects a very high standard of integrity from all staff, so the correct thing to do in the circumstance would be to record the fact that you were late, irrespective of whether or not someone had seen you.

20 *Explanation*: our work should be organized so that it is equally possible for both men and women to complete it equally well.

21 *Explanation*: if drinking alcohol, even in your own time, affects your work, then it is something your employer may be concerned about.

22 *Explanation*: to agree with this statement risks the suggestion that you have prejudices against certain sorts of people, and such a suggestion might seriously undermine the chances of your application being successful.

23 *Explanation*: being aggressive is never appropriate at work, no matter the provocation.

24 *Explanation*: you should not take it personally or allow it to affect your personal feelings if someone fails to conform to the conventions of good manners by refusing to shake your hand.

25 *Explanation*: every employee and manager should be willing to agree with this statement and help ensure that there is no place for bullying at work.

26 *Explanation*: to raise your voice is to shout, and at work shouting is not appropriate behaviour.

27 *Explanation*: in every workplace jokes are told but it is implied in the statement that someone does not find the jokes funny. When this happens the joking should stop.

28 *Explanation*: to agree with this statement suggests that you are only just in control of your temper and may not always manage to control it. To admit this would not support your application for a managerial position.

29 *Explanation*: to hold a grudge and seek revenge, as are implied in this statement, are not an appropriate way to behave in work. The correct thing to do if someone is upsetting you would be to tell them about how you feel, and if it continues, use the process described in the grievance procedure to resolve the issue.

30 *Explanation*: in some cultures it is normal to remove your shoes before entering a house and to refuse to do so or leave rather than do so would suggest an insensitivity towards practices and traditions different from your own.

Answers and explanations for Chapter 5

Warm-up questions for the data-interpretation test

1 A, Brian will not be 45 until his birthday the next day.

2 D, the difference between 1985 and 1955, both being born on the same day.

3 D, the only time when Brian and James were both aged four is between 17.01.1964 (James's fourth birthday) and 01.02.1964 (the eve of Brian's fifth birthday).

4 B, if the difference is equal to 25%, then £15.00 must be 75%. Therefore £15.00/3 = 25% = £5.00.

5 E, air, commodity and ship brokers have the lowest percentage increase, at 22.0%.

6 E, for 2001: total earnings = £1,000,685, average earnings = £1,000,685/20 = £50,034.25. For 1991: total earnings = £617,395, average earnings = £617,395/20 = £30,869.75. Therefore 2001 average – 1991 average = £50,034.25 – £30,869.75 = £19,164.50.

7 D, to be ranked first, air traffic planners and controllers must earn at least £110,342 in 2001 (£1 more than general managers). This would be an increase from their 1991 earnings of (£110,342 – £27,476)/£27,476 × 100 = 301.6%.

8 C, an increase of 166.3% would produce a salary of £47,007, placing professional athletes 8th, above industrial underwriters and claims assessors, but below doctors.

9 D, growth in earnings increased by £11.40 between 1989 and 1990, higher than any other year.

10 E, £353.40 – £227.60 = £125.80.

11 A, £353.40 – £259.70 = £93.70/£259.70 × 100 = 36.1%.

12 B, average non-manual men's wages (£285.46) – average manual men's wages (£205.23) = £80.23.

13 C, addition of the 1991 figures for higher, further and adult education (£3,734 million) + polytechnics and Colleges Funding Council (£993 million) = £4,727 million.

14 F, £8,287 million – £5,523 million = £2,764 million/£5,523 million × 100 = 50.0%.

15 E, Total expenditure (£34,041 million) = 5.1% of GDP. Therefore (£34,041/5.1) × 100 = £667,471 million.

16   B, VAT amount (£2,705 million)/subtotal of expenditure before VAT (£21,913 million + £2,678 million) = £24,591 million = 11.0%.

17   D, the range between lowest low water (1.0 m) and highest high water (9.3 m).

18   A, average low-water height throughout the week for mornings is 1.8 m; for afternoons it is 1.9 m.

19   F, care must be taken when calculating time. The length of sunlight must be calculated as part of the 60-minute clock. Therefore, if sunset was at 18:59 (two minutes earlier than recorded), the daylight hours would be: 18:59 – 05:23 = 13 h 36 m, plus the two minutes to 19:01 = 13 h 38 m.

20   E, a high tide 35 minutes before Liverpool would bring the Liverpool high tide in the afternoon into the morning at Southport, ie 12:16 – 35 = 11:41.

21   C, to find the median, simply put the values in size order, the median value is the middle one.

22   E, find the range by subtracting the lowest number from the highest, but if the lowest number is a negative, then remember – – = +, so add the negative number to the highest to find the distance between the two values.

23   A, there is nothing approximate about the answer. The suggestion that the answer may only be a close representation was included so as to undermine you. Unfair? Not really: you should show decisiveness and clarity of mind when the data are confused or even misleading. Find the 2005 value, then find the increase. The value has increased 1.6%, so 101.6% = 406,400; 1% = 406,400/101.6 = 4,000, so the investment in 2005 = 100 × 4,000 = 400,000; the increase was $6,400.

24   C, this is one for the calculator. You should be able to see that the answer is either UK or US shares and so need only undertake these calculations. It is wrong to simply work out the percentage change of the 2006 value, as this is the value after the increase. You must first find the value before the increase. In the case of US shares, 109.8% = 1,976,400, so the sum at the start of 2006 = 1,800,000 and the sum made was $176,400, while the sum made on UK shares was $175,200.

25   F, the value of the investment at the end of 2006 is £700,000, and the formula for the compound interest earned is F. Formula D would provide the final value of the fund.

26   B, if you answered C you shared a common misunderstanding that is worth getting right without wasting time on working it through. The company may triple the net profit but it will increase by 200% (because you have to subtract the percentage that you started with). For instance, 0.35 × 3 = 1.05, 0.35 × 200% = 0.7 (plus the original 0.35) = 1.05.

27   E, first calculate the net profit per unit sold, then calculate the net profit for Want to Be. $9.99 – retail commission and all costs of sales = $0.35 per unit × 2 million = $700,000.

28   B, first calculate the odds for buying a unit manufactured by Competitor: 30% = 0.3, then multiply (the events should be treated as independent) by the probability of it being faulty = $0.3 \times 0.1 = 0.03$.

29   B, first calculate the range of data – the sales figures for the three companies – and then calculate the mean. Want to Be's 2 m sales = 10% of the market, so the range is 2 m + 6 m + 12 m = 20 m ÷ 3 = 6.6 (to one decimal point).

30   D, the business model is dated 2006, so in 2002 it had been in use for four years. $9.99/(1.05)4 = $9.99 ÷ 1.05 = $9.514 ÷ 1.05 = $9.061 ÷ 1.05 = $8.629 ÷ 1.05 = $8.218 = $8.22.

Warm-up questions for the verbal test

Passage 1

1   A, the blue line is described as running north–south and the red line runs east–west, so the angle at the point of intersection must be 90 degrees.

2   A, it is clear from the text that the blue line runs north–south and the red line east–west. It is also said that the green line intersects the red line east of the blue line and the grey line intersects the blue line south of the red line. This means that the grey line would intersect the red line west of the green line.

3   B, as the blue line runs north–south, the intersections of the yellow and green lines with the blue line will take place at the same east–west position.

4   C, there is no information contained within the text to indicate the starting or end positions of the lines.

Passage 2

5   B, it is clear from the text that the eurozone rate is expected to remain unchanged.

6   A, it is stated that the yen's recent strength is not sustainable.

7   C, it is unclear from the passage whether or not the two currencies are at present aligned or will continue to be.

Passage 3

8   A, as Team 4 has won more games than Team 1 and has not lost any games, Team 4 must have more points than Team 1 as they have played the same number of games.

9   B, team 3 has seven more points than Team 2 and Team 6 has four more points than Team 2. This means that Team 3 has three more points than Team 6.

10   C, although it can be proved from the passage that Team 2 will have fewer points than any other of the teams listed, we do not know how many teams there are in the league. This means that it is possible there are other teams in the league and that they may have fewer points than Team 2.

Passage 4

11 C, the passage makes no comment on this issue.
12 A, this can clearly be seen from the passage.
13 B, the principal point concerns the enhancement of a manager's decisions by the incorporation of tests in the overall decision-making process.

Passage 5

14 A, this answer is clearly correct from the passage.
15 A, because it rains consecutively on a Friday/Saturday there are only three days that follow rain but on which it does not rain. We also know that two of these days must be Sundays. As there are two occasions on which the sky is clear all day after the rain, at least one of these must be a Sunday.
16 C, this is only true if it rains on the first Wednesday and the first Friday. As the passage does not identify which days it rains on each week, we cannot confirm that this is true.

Passage 6

17 B, you also need to meet the earnings requirement.
18 A, 17.5% of £30,000 = £5,250.
19 A, the passage states that all contributions qualify for tax relief at the highest rate paid by the saver.

Passage 7

20 A, it is stated that the bedrooms are on the second floor and the kitchen/family room is on the third.
21 C, the size of the reception room is not given.
22 A, while the text does not state which floor the reception room is on, it can be deduced that it is on the first, because it is the only floor not described.

Passage 8

23 B, a keyboard can be used to input to a command interface but it is not a command interface.
24 A, it is clear from the text that application software consists of user-related programs.
25 A, the passage states that the user interface is such a means of communication and it is also described as the human–computer interface.

Passage 9

26 A, the passage clearly states that the velocity and displacement of straight-line motion can be attributed negative values.

27 C, the rules of dynamics are not covered in the passage.

28 B, the statement is true with respect to the forces that act on the particle but is false overall because the passage makes clear that the discipline is not limited to the study of particle motion in straight lines.

Passage 10

29 A, Australia is in the southern hemisphere, so depressions would generate winds in the opposite direction to the anticlockwise winds of a northern-hemisphere depression.

30 A, the passage states that winds in depressions are revolving. As a depression passes the town, therefore, it would experience winds in opposite directions on either side of the depression. This would be the experience in either hemisphere.

31 B, in the northern hemisphere it would be your left ear; in the southern hemisphere it would be your right.

Passage 11

32 B, the insurance broker is on the same side of the road as the off-licence, while the pharmacist is on the same side as the newsagent. It is clear, therefore, that they are not on the same side of the road, as the newsagent is described as directly opposite the off-licence.

33 A, the bus stop is across the road from the optician, which in turn is across the road from the pharmacist. This means that the bus stop and the pharmacist are on the same side of the road.

34 B, there is a two-shop gap between the post office and off-licence, and this gap is in part taken up by either the clothes shop or butcher. In either event this leaves insufficient space for the optician and insurance broker. This means that the optician cannot be next to the butcher.

Passage 12

35 C, the work would end in the right-hand corner only if the worker started each line of boards in the left-hand corner, but the instructions only state that the first line is started in this way.

36 A, the end board will be cut to fit the space that remains, and is likely to result in a longer or shorter leftover piece. This is to be used to start the next row so long as the difference in lengths is greater than 50 cm.

37   A, as the board is described as having a long and a short side, you can deduce that the short end of the board can be called its end.

Passage 13

38   B, the passage states that it takes Steve less time than James to get to the meeting and that it takes James 9 minutes, so the statement must be false.

39   A, as it takes James longer to get to the meeting than Steve or Helen, and he sets off after Helen, he must arrive after she does.

40   C, although Richard has to travel further, we have no indication of how long his journey will take and so whether he would need to set off first in order to arrive first.

Answers and explanations for Chapter 6

Practice test 1: data interpretation

Situation 1

1   C, all the other periods have at least one subsidized session during the month.

2   B, Addison, Baldock, Clark, Edwards, Gordon, Humphreys, Isaacs, Jordan, Lloyd, Milton, Newton and Orwell all pay full rate: 12 @ £5.00 = £60.00. Dickinson, Fitch and Keith all have subsidized sessions: 3 @ £2.50 = £7.50. Humphreys has a solo extra lesson: 1 @ £6.00 = £6.00. Clark and Gordon share an extra lesson: 2 @ £3.50 = £7.00. Therefore: £60.00 + £7.50 + £6.00 + £7.00 = £80.50.

3   D, starting at 13.00: No change; remains Milton (M). 13.30: revised to Orwell (O). 14.00: No change; remains Lloyd (L). 14.30: revised to Edwards (E). 15.00 and 15.30 cancelled.

4   C, £212.00/£4.00 = 53 tickets sold by 15 people = 3.5 tickets per person.

Situation 2

5   B, old rates: £180 (early July) + £230 (late July) = £410. Minus new rates: £140 (early July) + £180 (late July) = £320. Therefore the saving is £410 – £320 = £90.

6   A, £65.00 (new tax) – £42.00 (old tax) = £23.00 × 6,731 (fares sold) = £154,813.

7   D, old price: £200 (July) + £250 (August)) = £450. New price: £150 (July) + (200 – 25% = £150) (saving in August) = £300. Saving: £450 – £300 = £150.

8   C, although the increase in price for Tenerife is the largest (£100), it is not the greatest percentage increase. Lanzarote: new fare £275 (August) – £180 (July)

= £95/£180 × 100 = 52.78%. Tenerife: new fare £300 (August) – £200 (July) = £100/£200 × 100 = 50.00%.

Situation 3

9 D, £356.16 × 48 months = £17,095.68.

10 C, Repayment of £154.21 × 60 months = £9,252.60 + £598.80 difference = £9,851.40.

11 B, 24 months at £454.98 will cost Mr Patel £10,919.52; all the others will cost him more overall.

12 F, without the disclosure of the variable administration fee, this figure cannot be calculated.

Situation 4

13 D, other industries. Three sets of data increase (road transport, other industries and residential); from the graph you can estimate that other industries saw the largest relative (percentage) increase, from 27 to 29 million tonnes.

14 D, the levels of emission are 63:27, which simplifies to 7:3.

15 C, you are asked to calculate what year emissions were approximately 20 million tonnes if they grew 10% a year prior to 1993. As with most questions, there are a number of ways to approach this question. One is to start with 20 and calculate a 110% increase to establish a four-year total of 29.282. 1993 – 4 = 1989.

16 D, 50% 2007 levels of emissions from road and residential (total 54.82 million tonnes ÷ 2) = 27.41; total 2007 emissions = 100% = 153.46; – 27.41 = 126.05. Estimate the percentage equivalent of the fraction 126.05/153.46, eg = 125/150 = 5/6 = 83%, a reduction of 17%, so answer is between 15 and 20%.

Situation 5

17 E, the rate has decreased; to express that decrease as a percentage: 0.021 ÷ 100 = 0.00021, 0.01995 ÷ 0.00021 = 95; therefore change = –5%.

18 A, you must calculate a 4% increase on 0.055: 0.055 × 104% = 0.0572, so answer A.

19 C, today's rate has decreased by 6% on yesterday; you must find 94% of 0.00084: 0.00084 × 94% = 0.0007896, answer C.

20 D, in an export-dependent economy a strengthening of the currency would help hold inflation down, not fuel it. Street protests would not normally strengthen a currency, and outflows of money would normally be expected to weaken a currency.

Practice test 2: verbal test

Passage 1

1   B, the passage does not conclude that the internet has made policing of coursework impossible.

2   A, it is correct to describe between 20% and 60% as significant. You might describe the extent of plagiarism or cheating as a scandal but not the percentage of marks that are achieved through home-completed assignments.

3   D, in the passage, reference is made to a review and, at one point, the view of candidates is provided in quotation marks. This is sufficient for us to conclude that the passage relies on the findings of an investigative study. Comparative assertions are simply qualified statements.

4   B, the passage comments on examinations in which home-completed assignments contribute to the grade awarded. It is not reasonable therefore to draw conclusions about vocational qualifications which may or may not include home-completed assignments that contribute to grades.

Passage 2

5   B, the passage states that every person at risk can gain considerable benefits from the treatment, and the statement is false because it says *not* every person.

6   C, the claim is about the risk of a vascular event and not about the risk of cancer. So the correct answer must weaken the link between a lower risk of a heart attack resulting from the treatment in people with less than the highest levels of cholesterol. Only C does this by suggesting that the reduced risk is relatively small, rather than not much lower as claimed in the question.

7   B, reference to a third relates to the group most at risk of an attack. It is stated in the passage that new evidence suggests that patients with less than very high levels of cholesterol will also experience a significant drop in their cholesterol levels and a consequent lower risk of a vascular event.

8   A, the benefits are directly proportional to the size of reduction in cholesterol levels, and therefore it can be inferred that when deciding who should benefit, doctors should consider the size of drop in cholesterol that can be achieved, rather than giving the treatment to those with the highest initial levels.

Passage 3

9   B, the main theme of the passage is the issue of domestic growth, and the issue of interest rate increases resulting from higher oil prices is examined in the context of what effect this might have on growth.

10   A, the author refers to the stable job market and (consequent) increases in income and wages as the factors that will give rise to domestic growth on or above the long-term trend.

11 A, the passage states that for the forecast to be realized, household spending and domestic consumption would need to increase noticeably.

12 E, the passage states that most economists agree with the monetary policy of ignoring the first-round impact of this rise in the price of oil and waiting for any domestic second effect – higher prices in the shops – before taking action. Therefore the author would not agree with any of the suggested answers.

Passage 4

13 B, the answer is false because it is stated in the passage that an increase in train-journey miles is forecast.

14 C, the passage refers to governments rather than any particular government, which suggests that the area discussed includes more than one country; but no indication is given of which countries the passage relates to.

15 B, the passage does not mention journey times or higher fares.

16 D, the passage states: 'The paucity of public investment raises considerable doubts whether those few projects that are currently supported will ever be completed, because ministers are refusing to say how much public money they will receive.' But which type of projects are supported is not detailed.

Passage 5

17 C, the passage supports a description of the challenge as a predicament because whatever action is taken will have negative consequences.

18 D, only D is mentioned explicitly as a solution to fuel shortages; the others are factors or alternatives that may not eventuate.

19 E, fiscal policy concerns the way governments spend and tax in order to achieve goals; this topic is covered in the passage in terms of the Chinese policy of keeping the price of oil products artificially low. International relations between Russia and China are touched upon in the passage, as are the topics of fuel exports and retail price of diesel at the pump. But rationing is not discussed.

20 True, this is explicitly stated in the passage.

Passage 6

21 A, a careful reading of the passage shows that sequencing is indeed only mentioned in the passage in relation to the work of the Human Genome Project.

22 A, it is stated that the mapping of human genetic differences will hasten the identification of new ways to treat common ailments. It can be inferred that this will be possible because the map will accelerate the search for genes involved in common diseases. B and C are explicitly stated in the passage.

23   B, new treatments and diagnostic tests are mentioned in the passage, but preventative therapies are not touched upon.

24   B, it is the claim that some of our genetic differences explain our propensity for particular diseases that supports the conclusion that some of us enjoy good health, while others are more susceptible to many common diseases.

Passage 7

25   C, the main claim of the passage is that our criminal system is failing to prevent reoffending. This claim is premised on the assumption that the prevention of reoffending is the principal objective of the criminal system.

26   B, the reason given for abandoning programmes of education and rehabilitation is overcrowding.

27   A, answer D refers only to young offenders and the passage is not so limited. C's reference to rehabilitation programmes is inconsistent with the position taken in the passage. Sentence A has the same urgent tone adopted in the passage and is consistent with the passage's main theme. 'Recidivism' means to go back to crime and levels of recidivism will not decline as long as our punishments fail to deter further offences.

28   C, the reason given for the lack of rehabilitation provision is overcrowding, but the criminal system's willingness or otherwise to provide resources for such provision is not discussed in the passage, nor can it be inferred.

Passage 8

29   A, had the government been putting these contributions aside for the benefit of the pension holders, then (assuming that the pensions are self-funding) there is no reason why the contributions should not be available to meet the commitments.

30   D, the passage states that 12 million are directly affected but also that the large numbers of people who contribute only a small amount to a private pension scheme are also at risk.

31   C, the age of the migrants is not given and the pensioner–worker ratio would only be improved if the migrants were workers rather than pensioners.

32   B, the passage concludes on the subject of workers with inadequate private pension schemes, and therefore the follow-on sentence is most likely to be on that subject. Suggested answers B and D are the only sentences that continue that theme. But D can be rejected because no reference is made in the passage to long-awaited proposals on how to resolve the crisis.

Passage 9

33   A, the estimates of spending against tax raised suggests a significant deficit.

34   A, that independence might involve significant challenges does not mean that it cannot be afforded. The price of independence might (or might not) be high, but the Scottish people may be willing to afford it.

35   D, Scotland, Ireland and Sweden are comparable in terms of population and geographic location in Europe, but the passage does not concern itself with this issue. It is reasonable to surmise that an independent Scotland would derive a greater percentage of its tax revenue from oil, and therefore that its economy would be more closely tied to that sector than currently.

36   C, the passage only states the level of tax revenue if Scotland were to be allocated the entire tax take from this sector. No information is provided on whether or not this is likely to occur should Scotland achieve independence.

Passage 10

37   A, the passage states that youth unemployment is at a record level, so it can be taken to be at a level higher than in 1997.

38   E, the passage states that opponents would place far greater emphasis on the family unit as one that comprises a married couple, both of whom are living with their children, which would equally apply to gay couples caring for children and living in civil partnerships. The opponents' concept of family would therefore include married couples or couples living in a civil partnership with children. None of the suggested answers includes both these groups.

39   C, the date on which this allowance was abolished is not stated in the passage, nor can it be inferred from the passage.

40   D, the opponents are not against social cohesion but the ills that continue despite greater prosperity.

Further information

A great deal of information is available on the internet, and any search for terms such as UK government, UK Civil Service or Fast Stream will bring up many useful sites.

Job opportunities

All administrative grades:
- Jobcentre online: www.jobcentreplus.gov.uk/
- Civil Service Recruitment Gateway: www.careers.civil-service.gov.uk/index

Information on Fast Stream:
- www.faststream.gov.uk

The European Fast Stream:
- www.europeanfaststream.gov.uk

The GCHQ Fast Stream:
- www.gchq.gov.uk/recruitment/careers/

The Welsh Assembly Government Fast Stream:
- www.newydd.cymm.gov.uk/about/career_opportunities/fast_stream/

The Scottish Parliament Fast Stream:
- www.careers-scotland.org.uk/publicserviceadministrationfaststreamcivilservice

Information on the work of government:
- www.direct.gov.uk

Government Statistical Service:
- www.statistics.gov.uk

The Home Office:
- www.homeoffice.gov.uk

Free online practice tests can be found at:
- www.shl.com
- www.psl.com
- www.mikebryon.com